# PLAY ACTIVITIES
# FOR
# BOYS AND GIRLS

# PLAY
# FOR BOYS AND GIRLS

## A GUIDE FOR

OTHER BOOKS BY THE AUTHOR

SQUARE DANCES OF TODAY

RECREATION LEADER'S HANDBOOK

# ACTIVITIES

# (SIX THROUGH TWELVE)

## TEACHERS, PARENTS, AND RECREATION LEADERS

### RICHARD KRAUS
*Associate Professor, Department of Health Education,*
*Physical Education, and Recreation*
*Teachers College, Columbia University*

McGRAW-HILL BOOK COMPANY, INC.

NEW YORK   TORONTO   LONDON   1957

II

35399

TO
LISA AND ANDY
JANE AND MICHAEL

# PREFACE

From the centuries-old concept of play as a frowned-upon frivolity, we Americans have come in the past few decades to a full realization of its healthful and educational values. Today we recognize that one of the most important factors in bringing about physical, social, emotional, and intellectual growth and well-being at any age is a full, engrossing recreational life. This is doubly true for children, who are in their most formative years, since they normally have plenty of leisure time and a strong instinctive drive toward social play.

Many of us are just beginning to understand that children need help with their play activities. Too often they lack ideas, encouragement, and opportunity for the richest use of leisure time. It is up to all interested adults—whether they are parents or school teachers, church, camp, or community recreation leaders—to assist youngsters by encouraging and helping to guide better play activities and associations.

*Play Activities For Boys and Girls* is designed to assist such interested adults by offering them as much of the technical know-how and as many of the varied skills and activities as can be provided within the pages of a single volume. Its attempt to provide helpful suggestions for leadership and specific stunts and experiences in music, dramatics, games, dancing, and other creative and traditional areas should be especially valuable for those adult leaders who do not wish to, or cannot, build an extensive library of source books. For those who do wish to purchase additional, specialized books in various areas of children's play, an up-to-date list of approved books in these different categories is included in the back of this book.

The author wishes to thank Professor John Hutchinson and Professor Clifford L. Brownell, of the Department of Health Education, Physical Education, and Recreation, at Teachers College, Columbia University, and

Dr. S. J. Prezioso, Miss Vivian O. Wills, and Miss Bette Butterworth, of the Westchester County Recreation Commission, for their continued interest and support. To several reviewers of the manuscript during its throes of development, notably Miss Virginia Musselman of the National Recreation Association, goes sincere and deep-felt appreciation of their honest and valid criticism. Mrs. Deborah Hunt Jennings deserves credit for the musical accompaniments, and Carl Pfeufer for the illustrations.

Finally, as in *Recreation Leader's Handbook,* the author wishes to acknowledge his continuing debt to the many recreation leaders who, working with children, have evolved the activities and approaches described in this book and made them free to all—a joyous source of better and happier living for children, and a vital instrument in the making of better adults.

RICHARD KRAUS

# CONTENTS

## Part Two. A World of Play Activities

PART ONE

# GUIDING
# CHILDREN'S PLAY

# CHAPTER 1

# THE ROLE
# OF PLAY

All over the world, and at every age, children take part in play activities. My child and your child—and the youngsters next door. Watch them! In the country, on hard city streets, in settlement houses or after-school play centers, in home basements or attics, and during school recesses, play is a vital part of their lives.

The forms are many! Some play activities are passed down from generation to generation, from the older kids on the street to the toddlers. Others emerge as part of our modern era. Whatever the activities are, children usually take part in them spontaneously and happily.

Why is this so? Why do children play—and why is a varied, absorbing play life essential to the fullest and happiest growth of each child's personality?

## Why Do Children Play?

Ask a psychologist this question, and he is likely to reply, "Play comes as a result of deep-seated human urges. It is the child's attempt to meet important needs for approval, achieve status with his fellows, and gain the kind of satisfaction that comes from successful accomplishment.

"Play may represent an escape from boredom or conflict. It may be a gradual preparation for the later activities of adult life. Sometimes it is just an aimless expenditure of excess energy. Taken as a whole, it is the child's attempt to experiment with the world around him, to find out about his fellow human beings, and to discover his own abilities and interests. Play has all these reasons for being."

3

Play tells us a great deal about the essential nature of each child.

Ruth Strang has written, "The play life of a child is an index of his social maturity and reveals his personality more clearly than any other activity." [1]

Play is a major concern throughout childhood, and nature plants strong play drives in every normal child to satisfy certain basic needs of development. Children do not play because they are too lazy to work. Instead, they often put forward their greatest efforts and concentration in play activities and gain satisfaction and enthusiasm which no other experiences provide.

Gesell and Ilg have written, "Deeply absorbing play seems to be essential for full mental growth. Children who are capable of such intense play are most likely to give a good account of themselves when they grow up." [2]

Needless to say, children do not think of play as analytically as this. Ask the average youngster why he plays, and he is likely to answer simply, "Because it's fun. I enjoy it."

Or, as he fumbles for a deeper reason, "I play with my friends. We have a club and we do a lot of things together."

Or, "I like to be good at things. It's fun when they come out right. And sometimes I like to play alone, working on my collection, or in the shop."

Or possibly the most revealing answer of all, "Why do I play? Are you kidding? Everybody plays!"

## How Play Contributes to Child Growth

What are the chief ways in which play experiences help children reach their fullest potentials as human beings? There are six areas which may be described:

1. Physical growth and development
2. Emotional expression and release
3. Healthy socialization
4. Experiences in creative expression
5. Learning skills and hobbies
6. Understanding environment

All these areas are closely interwoven, but in order to highlight certain aspects of each, they are dealt with separately.

*Physical Growth and Development.* In order to develop healthy, soundly functioning organic systems, a variety of motor skills, and such desirable qualities as coordination, grace, balance, endurance, and speed, children should have plenty of opportunity for vigorous physical play.

With very young children, this will involve aimless crawling at first; then walking, running, tumbling, and climbing. These general skills become refined, as children learn narrower, more demanding skills. Through neighborhood games such as tag, chase, and relays, they develop more highly coordinated abilities in dodging, leaping, throwing, and catching. Eventually, as their over-all physical abilities develop, they may take part in team and dual sports and creative bodily activities, which prepare them for the demands of adolescent and adult life.

In brief, the major purposes of physical play are to achieve basic muscular strengths and coordinations; good postural habits and the ability to relax; the capacity for sustained effort, when necessary; development of body poise and grace; development of interest in maintaining one's own optimum physical, mental, emotional, and social well-being; development of courage, initiative, alertness, and cooperation in group activities and individual games.

With regard to the element of physical fitness, a recent study showed dramatically that American children are seriously inferior to European youngsters in certain tests having to do with strength and flexibility.[3] Although this study has been questioned by physical education authorities in the United States, there can be no question that the inactive lives many of our children lead are responsible for weakness and poor neuromuscular skills. Active, enjoyable programs of physical play represent an excellent way of meeting this problem and improving the fitness of American youth.

*Emotional Expression and Release.* Play activities should consistently help children meet their basic needs for approval, affection, emotional response from others, and group acceptance and status. If these needs are met sufficiently in play associations, each child is helped in becoming an emotionally secure person.

Further, through his play experiences the youngster should have an opportunity to release his tensions and aggressions in an unashamed, socially acceptable manner. Through forceful participation in sports and games, through role-playing in dramatic games and creative rhythms, and through enjoyable artistic expression, the child may be helped to "get it out of his system" and to voice his hidden feelings, either verbally or through bodily movement. Also, through such projective experiences he should become better able to understand and accept himself.

*Healthy Socialization.* Young children tend to be self-centered and primitive in their social behavior; pushing and pulling, grabbing, tearing, and tugging are often seen in nursery schools. However, as they grow up, youngsters learn to exist as members of a group. They take turns with equipment and games, recognize the needs and wishes of others, assume roles of leading or following, and accept and live up to responsibility, when necessary. Thus they gradually become cooperative social beings.

One of the richest laboratories for these important learnings is in the rough-and-tumble of the child's play life. This is especially true because, during the preadolescent gang age the child's relation to his peers, or equals, is so important to him. The peer group, composed of children of approximately the same age and background (and usually of the same sex), is the most vital social relationship in the child's life at this stage. Through it, he builds a society in which he can escape adult "do's" and "don'ts," establish values and rules of behavior, gain satisfactions, and mingle with friends who have similar goals and interests.

It is interesting to note that the less rewarding a child's life is, outside the peer group, the more a role within the group means to him. Bossard has written: [4]

> The boy and girl who have not succeeded in gaining a satisfactory status within their family . . . whose relations with their parents and other older people at home involves a constant struggle against domination or neglect . . . whose school achievements are nil or unsatisfactory . . . all these and many other types of frustrated and under-privileged children can find in peer groups, especially conflict gangs, the opportunity for individual achievement otherwise denied.

*Experiences in Creative Expression.* Until recently the principle was widely accepted that talent in the various art fields belonged to few individuals, and that most people could not, therefore, participate fruitfully in them in an active way.

Today it is believed that all children share creative impulses and the ability to take part in and enjoy creative expression. While every child may not turn out to be an artist (with a capital "A"), he has the potentiality for creative living, and deserves the kind of encouragement and stimulus that will give him enjoyable, broadening experiences in the various media of music, dramatics, drawing, painting, sculpture, dance, and the language arts. These experiences will give him greater pleasure in seeing the work of others, will enable him to be more sensitive and receptive to beauty and aesthetic qualities in all phases of his own life, and will provide him with hobby interests that may broaden and enrich his leisure-time life.

*Learning Skills and Hobbies.* When a child has experienced a wide range of play activities during his early years, many of these are likely to persist through maturity as a constant force for good mental health and an enriched, interesting life.

Jay Nash discovered, in a twenty-year survey of 1,000 graduate students,[5] that about 60 per cent of the hobby interests of these people had begun below the age of ten, and over 70 per cent, below the age of twelve. Only about 5 per cent of the hobbies listed were acquired after the age of twenty-one. Nash logically concluded that youth is the time to plant basic recreational interests.

Failure to acquire play interests in childhood may leave lasting gaps in later life. Although many adults regret that they never took up such activities as arts and crafts, music or dancing, when they were younger, research shows that for various reasons (lack of time or money, fear of failure, or slowness in learning) they find it difficult to add new pursuits once they are well into adulthood.

Another important factor is that of future vocational choices. Childhood play can give a youngster a first-hand knowledge of his own talents and abilities which will help him select his future occupation. How many successful commercial artists first drew on the cardboard that came in their fathers' shirts from the laundry—and how many big-league ballplayers first played sand-lot ball—all for sheer fun?

*Understanding Environment.* Through his play experiences, the child learns in a real and meaningful way about the world around him. He experiments with natural laws and with many different kinds of materials and play objects—including other children. He learns about gravity when he falls from a jungle gym, and about displacement of mass when a boxing glove with a fist in it hits him. Through leisure-time reading and dramatic play he may learn much about history and the people of other lands and centuries.

More and more, educators are coming to realize that a clear-cut line cannot be drawn between education and recreation. Through play the child gains intellectual growth; he stores away a wealth of facts and learns habits of disciplined thinking and problem solving. The chief purposes of education and play may differ—but their outcomes have much in common.

## Summary

This chapter discusses the role that play takes in the lives of children and outlines six chief areas in which it makes a major contribution.

# CHAPTER 2

# ACTIVITIES
# CHILDREN ENJOY

Which play activities do children enjoy the most? Which do they care little about? What determines a youngster's choice of recreational activities?

## Setting the Stage

Obviously, no six-year-old enters the world of play a complete novice. During the preschool years, he is likely to have become familiar with various kinds of toys and equipment, such as dolls; toy furniture, planes, boats, and cars; cutout and color-in picture books; swings; slides; see-saws; tricycles and pull wagons; wood blocks; sand; paper; paste; crayons; scissors; drums; rattles; phonograph records; and a host of other aids to fun.

Assuming that children have had satisfying "solo" and small-group experiences with such materials and equipment, they should have acquired a healthy variety of skills and play interests by the time they enter first grade. These are put to the test, expanded, and developed by the more highly socialized activities which absorb youngsters during the period between six and twelve. What are these activities?

## Childhood Play Activities

*Active Games and Sports.* This is the most widely found form of children's play. Why? The child's innate need for physical activity, the pleasure that he takes in vigorous movement, the excitement of chase and team play, and the mastery of personal physical powers, all add to its appeal. Young children enjoy games of tag, chase, and relays, and such simple

9

ball games as dodge ball or kick ball. They also take part in swimming, skating, and sledding. When they are about nine or ten, they begin to enjoy more complex team sports, such as volleyball, baseball, and basketball— although they will not be really skillful in these until they are in their teens. Self-testing activities such as tumbling stunts or gymnastics are of interest throughout this period.

*Inactive Games.* There are many social games and mixers which require little space for bodily movement and are therefore suitable for indoor play. These include dramatic games and stunts, mental and guessing games, so-called "magic" tricks, paper and pencil games, and equipment and board games.

## Creative Activities

Ideally, all play interests should be viewed as creative, in the sense that children approach them in an exploratory, spontaneous spirit. However, certain forms of play, usually having to do with the arts, are given this special title.

*Musical Play.* This includes recreational singing and musical games; also the use of simple instruments in rhythm bands. It is closely linked to rhythms, which involves the movement of children to musical or rhythmic accompaniment.

*Dance.* This may be divided into traditional dance (including singing games, play parties, folk, square, and ballroom dancing), and creative dance (including rhythms and expressive movement, which are very similar to modern dance or beginning ballet).

*Dramatic Play.* This includes charades, puppetry, pantomimes, shadow plays, informal skits and parodies, and dramatic storytelling, and may extend as far as actually presenting dramatic performances.

*Arts and Crafts.* These terms overlap, since every real art requires technique (craft) and every fine craft has elements of art. As they are commonly used, "art" refers to simple graphic and plastic experiences, like finger painting, the use of chalk, crayons, paints, clay and the like, while "craft" describes such skills as leather or metal working, weaving, carpentry, and ceramics.

## Hobby Activities

Hobbies include those pursuits which are voluntarily chosen and which are carried on in a sustained way, often requiring prolonged effort for satisfactory achievement. Usually they are enjoyed by individuals, in a self-absorbed way. A few examples:

Collecting, making model trains or planes, nature study, fishing and hunting, raising pets, gardening, cooking or sewing, science interests (astronomy, chemistry, or geology), and beginning business enterprises.

All of the play interests described in this chapter, as well as forms of passive amusement (like movies or television) represent important elements in the play lives of children. The most significant kinds, particularly those which adults may guide and stimulate, are described in Part Two of this book.

Children do not all participate equally in all sorts of activities, nor do all activities appear at all ages. What are the key factors underlying children's choices of play activities?

## Why Children Select Activities

*Family.* Parents and older brothers and sisters often influence children's choices through their examples and the encouragement or disapproval they show toward certain activities.

*School.* Children may wish to go further with play activities that have been enjoyed in school or to avoid those which were frustrating or boring.

*Sex.* During the gang age, children's play choices are affected by their sex allegiance. Boys are apt to like vigorous, combative games and sports activities and play having to do with construction, war, Western themes, etc. Girls usually prefer homemaking play having to do with playing house, caring for children, and cooking and sewing; they also enjoy art, music, and dance. Girls mature before boys do, as a rule, and therefore tire earlier of childhood games.

*Geography.* The terrain, climate, and other local factors influence play choices; the Southern youngster will have little chance to ski or ice-skate, while the boy on an Arizona desert will not know much about "skin-diving."

*Season.* Many sports are assigned to definite seasons of the year, like football in the fall, and baseball in the spring and summer. Others, like marbles and kite flying, seem to arrive at definite dates, which children are aware of and obey almost like clockwork.

*Social Pressure.* The high status value of success in a certain activity may encourage children to take part in it. Even when there is no special prestige to be gained, they are likely to "go along with the gang," whether or not they enjoy it particularly. National fads may also briefly influence children's play interests.

*Age.* A child's changing age often affects his play choices. Dramatic play and "make-believe," which is greatly enjoyed by preschool and primary grade children, declines steadily among children in the intermediate grades, who have become more interested in real-life situations. Until the age of nine or ten, children take part in an increasing number of different activities (some youngsters may enjoy as many as a hundred different forms of play in a week). Then it begins to lessen in variety as children consolidate their interests and probe more deeply into those of greatest appeal. With increasing age children are attracted to more and more complex activities as well as those requiring group cooperation on a higher level.

*Personality.* Probably the most important factor is that each child selects pursuits in terms of his own physical structure and abilities, and his psychological and social make-up and needs.

## Surveys of Children's Play Interests

Two interesting surveys were carried out with large groups of children, which reflect their preferences and attitudes about play. Brief outlines of these surveys follow.

### "WHAT WE LIKE TO DO"

The New York State Education Department, through its Bureau of Physical Education, questioned over 1,500 boys and girls in the fourth, fifth, and sixth grades, in twenty-three rural and urban schools, about their preferences in the broad area of sports and games.[6]

*Activity Preferences.* Swimming was the most highly valued activity; bicycling, hiking, archery, and roller-skating were also highly valued. Wrestling and boxing were enjoyed by boys; and badminton and tennis, by both sexes. Both boys and girls enjoyed softball and volleyball; the latter was scored somewhat higher by girls.

Both sexes enjoyed using equipment like "jungle gyms" and flying rings. Boys gave a higher score to chinning and rope climbing, and girls preferred doing cartwheels. The ability to catch a ball was rated highly by both sexes. Both boys and girls showed much concern about good posture and ways of improving it.

Under the heading of dancing, over 50 per cent of the boys enjoyed both square and social dancing, and a much higher percentage of girls. Folk dancing, which demands more intricate skills, was less popular with boys, although girls gave it a high ranking. In the game category, both sexes showed interest in tag and chase games, although girls who had reached the age of twelve showed lessened approval of these childhood pastimes. Activities like jacks, hopscotch, and rope jumping were primarily enjoyed by girls, and boys were somewhat more interested in horseshoe pitching.

*General Attitudes about Play Participation.* In response to questions on "how we play games," a number of interesting reactions appeared. Children felt that it was important to be able to play different positions and to be given a chance at refereeing or being captain. They agreed that everyone in the class should have the right to play on teams, rather than just the best players. Most of the girls and about two-thirds of the boys felt that boys and girls should sometimes play together on the same teams. They agreed that it was not essential to be on a winning team at all times, and that teams should be "fairly" chosen, so every person has a chance to win.

Both sexes expressed a strong need for more time, teacher assistance, space, and equipment for play.

## "THE INTEREST FINDER"

Arthur Jersild and Ruth Tasch also conducted a study of children's interests that was broader than the New York State survey, both in terms of the information sought and the age range of the children investigated. The report of their findings, *Children's Interests and What They Suggest for Education,* was published in 1949.[7] It covered material gained by surveying over 3,000 children from first grade through senior high school, primarily in Springfield, Missouri, but also in several schools in the South and Northeast.

The survey indicated:

The range of children's out-of-school play interests is very limited when compared with their potentialities. Many youngsters spent a great deal of free time in repetitive and unproductive activity in which they did not seem to be greatly interested, and often expressed boredom.

In most communities there is little relation between the activities children are most preoccupied with *in* school and those they carry on *outside* school. There was very little mention of intellectual, artistic, or cultural interests, or of constructive hobbies in children's accounts of their out-of-school activities.

Many parents restrict themselves to a limited range of activities when they spend free time with their children and seem to have a limited conception of the possibilities in the community for cultivating children's interests. Parents are pleased by interests their children develop, but tend to regard them passively and do little to foster them.

What conclusions may be drawn from these two studies?

The most obvious one is that, if children are to have rich and satisfying play lives, they need the constant encouragement and assistance of interested parents, teachers, and recreation leaders.

## Summary

This chapter describes various types of childhood play, and outlines some of the factors underlying children's choices of different interests. Two surveys of children's activities are summarized, one having to do with physical education preferences, and the second with the total range of children's interests. Need is expressed for schools, community agencies, and parents to join together to promote and improve the play life of children.

# CHAPTER 3

# HOW ADULTS CAN HELP

"All well and good," the average parent or classroom teacher is likely to say at this point. "But what can I do about improving children's recreation activities? Why, the children I know don't *like* interference! They want to play by themselves. . . ."

It is true that a great deal of children's play is carried on in small, temporary groupings of youngsters, who wish to remain free of adult domination. Provided that their activities are not antisocial, there is no need to control or "interfere" with them, although it is entirely possible that they would *welcome* friendly adult interest and assistance. However, there are many special circumstances when children's play does require special adult guidance.

## When Is Help Needed?

When a children's play program is formally sponsored by an organization—be it church, community recreation department, or settlement house—with certain definite goals, responsible adult leaders should be placed in charge if these goals are to be reached. This is particularly true if problems of discipline or safety are involved.

When children's groups are formed to meet regularly over a period of time, mature guidance is needed to help the participants carry on a sustained, stable program. Youngsters are often so volatile that, if left completely to their own impulses, they might be likely to let minor crises break up their groups. As Ruth Strang has put it, "Skillful supervision encourages the children to plan their own activities and guides them just enough so that

15

they will have the satisfaction of reaching the group goal by working together." [8]

When any special event or complicated plan of action is being considered, such as a sports tournament, trip, play day, or festival, it will often be found that children need the help and guidance of experienced adults.

Finally, mature supervision is certainly necessary when the children taking part are "special," in the sense of being either physically handicapped or emotionally disturbed. Play experiences can be a great force for growth and recovery with such youngsters. But, obviously, sound judgment is needed in selecting activities that are within their range of achievement and that will contribute to their rehabilitation. Instructional skills and thoughtful, sensitive, day-by-day personal guidance are also essential.

Apart from these special circumstances, it must be realized that play in its finest form does not exist in a vacuum. Without help and inspiration, it may be a barren, uninteresting, or disorganized process. Jersild and Tasch revealed how often children's play was boring and repetitive to them. How often have we all seen youngsters hanging around street corners, aimlessly frittering their time away? Summer's end often comes as a relief to such children.

The need to provide fuller play opportunities today is underlined by the shifts that American society has undergone within recent decades. In the transition from rural to urban living, many changes have taken place, particularly with regard to family life. The family is not so solid a unit as in the past in terms of shared activities and interests, respect for parents, or continuity of generations living together. The incidence of divorce and broken homes is higher. At the same time that our advanced technology has given both children and adults more leisure time, the nature of our crowded living in cities and built-up suburbs has constricted their opportunities for enjoyable play. In everyday life there are many provocative stimuli that glamorize the cult of violence, brutality, and lurid sex, such as unsavory movies, television, and radio programs, comic books and semipornographic literature made readily available to children. To counteract these forces by providing constructive forms of play that will have comparable appeal to children is one of the major challenges facing recreation leaders—and all adults concerned with children's welfare—today.

## Contributions of Adult Leaders

What are the specific kinds of contributions that interested adults may make to children's play programs?

The adult leader may stimulate vital and interesting recreational experiences by suggesting new activities and offering needed equipment and materials. In addition to suggesting play activities, the adult leader may actually instruct the children in the skills and techniques involved.

As a group leader or counselor, the adult can help children improve their ways of getting along cooperatively, establishing constructive democratic values, and setting up realistic immediate and long-range goals. He can help them work out needed and acceptable rules of behavior and codes for enforcing these.

Each adult may make it his responsibility to awake community-wide consciousness of the need to sponsor desirable children's play programs. Within recent years a number of cities and towns have been trail blazers in establishing such activity programs. Here are a few examples:

The townspeople of Coral Gables, Florida, to commemorate their soldiers of World War II, chose to erect a fine War Memorial Youth Center. This attractive and useful building today provides sports, swimming, arts and crafts, dramatics, discussion groups, dancing, and refreshments for children from the first grade through high school. Since the Youth Center was built, juvenile delinquency, which had never been a serious threat in Coral Gables, declined by an additional healthy 30 per cent.[9]

Parents of Franklin Park, a section of suburban Santa Rosa, California, were worried about an old sawmill around which their children used to play, and which was a constant threat of accidents. Pitching in together, with all labor and materials donated by interested citizens, they built a big redwood clubhouse (valued at $20,000) at no cost to the city. People of many backgrounds pitched in together to tear down the old mill and erect the attractive clubhouse, which now houses many worthwhile recreation projects for children.[10]

There are many other examples of interested citizens getting together to organize advisory groups for recreation, and developing cooperative summer play schools, youth canteens, and the like.

## Settings for Guided Play

Recognizing the specific kinds of contributions adults may make, what are the settings in which guided play may be carried on? There are several kinds of sponsoring organizations, such as schools, community recreation departments, youth-serving organizations and associations, homes, hospitals or treatment centers for handicapped children, and camps.

### SCHOOLS

Schools represent a vital force today for the promotion of desirable play programs. Modern education is concerned with much more than transmitting a narrow cluster of academic skills and information; its ultimate goal is the child's becoming a well-adjusted, fully rounded, and capable adult citizen. John Dewey wrote, at a time when the value of play was less widely recognized than it is today: "Education has no more serious responsibility than making adequate provision for enjoyment of recreative leisure, not only for the fact of immediate health but still more, if possible, for the fact of its lasting effect on habits of the mind." [11]

In terms of an enriched curriculum, it is also accepted that playlike activities, which tend to motivate children highly, can also be used to impart vital educational outcomes. If, however, we accept the point of view that some distinction should be made between schoolwork and play, it might be stated in this way:

Work, or study, is a school experience in which the child's learning of academic knowledge or skills is considered to be the most important outcome.

Play, on the other hand, is something in which enjoyment is likely to be the chief outcome, but which has many other incidental values and possibilities for growth.

There are several ways in which play experiences may be provided in schools.

*Scheduled Play.* All children share a need for active physical play. This is recognized in many states which require, by statute, that a minimum amount of time be devoted to physical education each week. To satisfy this requirement, sports or games sessions are held in activity rooms, gymnasiums, or outdoor play areas; they are likely to be under the direction of a physical education specialist in some schools and classroom teachers in others.

*Free Periods.* There are usually a number of periods during the day when children are in and around the school, but when no instruction is scheduled for them. Such free time may be during recess, the lunch hour, or before or after classes (particularly when the school bus delivers children early, or when they have to wait for a time to be taken home). Usually during these noninstructional periods children gather in whatever space is available and take part in unregulated play.

There is always the likelihood that older, more confident children will monopolize the space and play equipment available at such times. To prevent this, Edwin Trethaway suggests [12] that play areas be so laid out and organized that children may voluntarily participate in special sections reserved for their age groupings. Trethaway comments that when it is recess (which may be considered an official part of the school day), too many teachers make a practice of just turning their pupils loose to play. Instead, he feels that the task of supervising the recreation area should be shared by classroom teachers, and that class units should be rotated from activity to activity from week to week. The difference between this and the regular physical education class is that there is no instruction during the recess hour (although youngsters may play games they first learned in the physical education class).

*Unscheduled Classroom Play.* There are often times during regular classroom hours when, because of mental strain, tension, or fatigue of one kind or another, teachers may feel it is desirable to provide brief play sessions right in the classroom. To clear the air and provide a relaxing atmosphere, this sort of play can be informally introduced; it may include games, dancing, singing, dramatics, or any of the enjoyable activities described in Part Two of this book.

*Special-interest Clubs.* Many schools officially sponsor regular times during the week when clubs based on the special interests of children may meet, usually with teacher advisers. These clubs may meet after school hours, although in some schools they are likely to be scheduled during the morning or early afternoon. The club program may involve sports or dancing (often classes in the latter skill are provided by Parent-Teacher Associations), or may be concerned with hobby areas, such as crafts, photography, or dramatics. While these clubs meet in the school, the atmosphere, pace, and teacher-child relationships in them tend to be less formal and more relaxed than in the ordinary classroom situation.

*Summer Play Programs.* Many schools have experimented in recent years with outdoor education, field trips, and utilizing camping experiences as a direct but informal means of achieving learning. A striking extension of this is in the use of the summer months as a time for voluntary attendance of children in school-sponsored activities which are geared toward both recreational enjoyment and academic growth.

One example of this is in the Public School Summer Enrichment Program of the State of Florida.[13] Written into state law in 1947 and made available to children throughout the state, this school-operated program does not offer formal academic instruction, but gives children an opportunity to take part in athletics, arts and crafts, camping, dramatics, excursions, homemaking (cooking, home decoration, clothing arts), library services, music, social recreation, and many special events. Those adults who hearken back to the joyous cry of "School's out!" that they heard in June during their own childhood, will be amazed to learn that as many as 125,000 children of a total state enrollment of 500,000 in Florida's public schools have voluntarily chosen to attend this summer program.

COMMUNITY CENTERS AND YOUTH-SERVING ORGANIZATIONS AND PROGRAMS

Beginning at the age of about eight, many youngsters begin to join formally organized clubs and to take part in activity programs sponsored by youth-serving organizations or carried on in community centers or municipal play areas. The total range of organizations which provide such play opportunitis includes the following: Boy and Girl Scouts, Camp Fire Girls, Boys Club of America, Boys Republic, Police Athletic League, Four-H Club, Grange and Farmer's Union youth groups, church clubs, Catholic Youth Organization, Young Men's and Young Women's Christian and Hebrew Associations, Play School Association, and municipally or privately sponsored playgrounds, playfields, and youth centers and canteens. Most of these organizations provide play for children in the preadolescent and adolescent stages of life, and a few even provide programs for preschool youngsters.

Programs sponsored by such organizations take many different forms. Here are several examples:

*Emphasis on Sports and Games.* Such organizations as the Catholic Youth Organization, Boys Club of America, and Police Athletic League conduct (among their many other activities for young people) city-wide sports and games programs, with emphasis on local teams competing against each other in tournaments and round robins. These activities serve an especially worthwhile function in slum areas where the tendency of youngsters to join antisocial street gangs may be diverted and compensated for in a wholesome way through sports competition.

Programs like Little League baseball which appeal to preteen youngsters, have, for the most part, been uncritically accepted by the American public. While it is true that this miniature version of big-league baseball is a colorful and challenging experience for highly skilled youngsters, and that it gives many adults the chance to work with boys and feel that they are contributing to the well-being of their communities, a number of basic criticisms have been voiced about it. Chiefly these have to do with the overemphasis on developing high degrees of skill and the danger of doing possible psychological damage to boys at this young, extremely impressionable age.

*Social Clubs.* Another type of group is the social club which meets regularly in a settlement house, "Y," or community center, without placing special emphasis on any particular form of activity or play interest. These are usually friendship clubs, homogeneous in nature, with children of approximately the same age, sex, and socioeconomic background, and often from the same school or neighborhood. Depending on the resources of the youngsters and the amount of stimulus and guidance given them, their program may be rich and diverse or disappointingly barren and boring.

*Hobby Groups.* Often clubs may meet to take part in hobby interests, such as photography, bowling, or model plane construction. These are not so likely to be homogeneous as friendship clubs are, since, on the surface at least, the members have been drawn together by a mutual play interest, rather than other ties. In this sort of interest group the leader may tend to assume the role of a teacher, since it is assumed that he has certain skills and he is in charge of the use of facilities and equipment.

*Free Play.* Another common pattern is to have free play available throughout a building or play area, offering a variety of quiet or strenuous activities. In such a setting children may pick and choose, without committing themselves for any set length of time to a single club or group. This type of program may be found in after-school, indoor play centers, or on summer playgrounds.

*National Youth Organizations.* A final type of program is that of the national youth organization which has a formal ritual and course of materials or activities, such as the Boy or Girl Scouts, with their various grades and ranks of membership, merit badges, and codes of behavior. Often such character-training organizations make extensive use of play activities at special times during their regular meetings or fun sessions.

Many of these recreation programs depend on adult volunteer leadership to a great extent, particularly in organizations like the Boy or Girl Scouts. There is an increasing need for parents and other adults to take on this type of community service. Recently Dorothy Barclay wrote, "In the five boroughs of New York City alone, 10,000 girls are on waiting lists for membership in Girl Scout troops. Just one thing holds up this big parade—a shortage of adult leaders." [14] On a nation-wide scale, the Girl Scouts aim to recruit 300,000 additional leaders within the next five years.

It has been pointed out that children who are younger than eight often do not have formal group affiliations of this kind, although they may take part in playground, community center, or playschool activities. For youngsters in the first three grades of school, therefore, the home and the neighborhood around it is an especially important center of play activity.

PLAY AT HOME

Assuming that there is sufficient space to serve this purpose, the home is an ideal informal setting for childhood play. It should afford a logical base of operations, particularly for younger children who cannot safely roam too far away. Parents should ensure that children have a rich opportunity for enjoyable, vital play, by providing the following:

*A Good Place to Play.* This may be a basement area, a special playroom, an outdoor area, or a bedroom or attic, where children may keep the toys, equipment, and materials that are needed in play, and where they may be as noisy and cluttered-up as they please. *Parents' Magazine* has published numerous articles on this theme.

*Equipment and Materials.* In addition to space, parents should provide as wide a variety as possible of toys, equipment, and supplies that are needed for play. There have also been many articles published on this subject in *Parents Magazine,* including several showing parents how to construct inexpensive equipment and toys.

*Encouragement.* The interested parent will encourage groups of youngsters to come together in the home to play, regularly if they wish it, or just on rainy days or special occasions if that seems to be what they want. Some parents display an attitude of "All right, go ahead and play—but don't bother me with it." James Hymes, Jr., points out that these adults are often not convinced of the worth of play because they have the outmoded idea that recreation is a worthless frivolity and because they themselves never truly learned to play wholeheartedly.[15] But today more and more parents have become truly hospitable in their homes toward groups of neighborhood children, partly because they recognize, in a narrow sense, that this may be helpful to their own child's popularity, and partly also because they genuinely appreciate the broad values inherent in desirable play activities.

*Mutual Participation.* Many parents may join their children in sharing play or hobby experiences. As an example, the article "What a Hobby Did for Our Son" [16] describes the experience of parents of a fifth-grade boy who took up the hobby of mineralogy. They found themselves joining him on field trips, visiting museums, and writing to geology societies for rock specimens from all forty-eight states. Before long, in order to keep up with him, they joined the state mineralogical society. Another couple took up the wonderful hobby of ham radio at the same time as their fourth-grade son. Like 120,000 other Americans (including many boys and girls as young as eight) who are permitted to obtain "Novice" ratings, they found themselves chatting with people all over the world on their own wavelength.[17] Various other forms of family fun activities are described in Chapter 14.

In general, parents must realize that it is important for children to get an abundance of security in their home environments if they are to be successful in group play with children of their own age. Zachry suggests that the young child who is not sure of the affections of his parents is likely to be reluctant to try himself out in a group of his age-mates. His readiness to move from the greater dependence of early childhood into this kind of exposed position stems from the basic security he is given at an early age by the adults who are closest to him.[18]

Another important aspect of the home in relation to children's play is that it is highly desirable that youngsters have a good deal of favorable contact with their male parent. Father's role, in the word's of B. D. Hendy, a British psychiatrist, is that of being ". . . a man in the world of men. He helps children realize the meaning of freedom, detachment and adventure. He should be a fund of knowledge, an organizer of expeditions and excursions, and one who brings interesting people and things into the home." [19] There is evidence that children growing up in home without an adult male show self-reliance, but also a general feeling of lack of personal worth, lack of faith in the future, and a "what's the use" attitude which leads to much difficulty in school. This seems to affect boys of nine to twelve most severely.

It is important for each youngster to know that his dad cares about him. Dorothy Barclay comments, "The youngster whose dad heads up an important P.T.A. committee, serves on the local scout council, turns out to clear a campsite or volunteers to coach swimming at the park pool knows without a doubt that his father thinks kids are worth working for." [20]

Since the home is where so much of the child's leisure time is spent, it is the parent, more than any other adult, who should be concerned about the possible effects of his child's absorption with "crime" or "horror" comics, or with radio or television programs that are concerned with violence or sex themes. Dr. Fredric Wertham and others have given wide publicity to the danger of this sort of influence,[21] although some authorities state that it cannot be proven that any youthful crime or personality disturbance finds its tap roots in this sort of stimulus. In any case, every thoughtful parent will attempt to minimize his child's absorption in this kind of recreational interest by guiding him along more constructive and positive lines.

## Play Activities for the Handicapped

In past years the tendency was to think of children with major disabilities as being quite apart from normal children—whether the disability involved a physical handicap or mental retardation.

Today it is believed that "exceptional" children are youngsters much like all others, each with his individual characteristics, capacities, interests, and possibilities for growth. As science teaches us more about their afflictions, and as new media of therapy are evolved, fuller, happier lives are emerging for the blind, orthopedically handicapped, cerebral-palsied, and mentally disturbed or retarded children of our nation. In this total picture play activities have a significant role.

Activities may be provided for children who have somewhat similar disabilities (thus establishing a similar scheme of limitations) in hospitals, clinics, and special school classes and camps. Or, when handicapped youngsters are reasonably able to participate on the same level with other, "normal" youngsters, they may be integrated with them, in order to help them avoid the deeply felt stigma of being totally "different."

Many colleges and universities have been preparing professional workers in this field, and such national organizations as the American Association for Health, Physical Education and Recreation and the National

Recreation Association have stimulated much interest in experimental studies and projects in the field of recreation in rehabilitation. Several examples of such ventures follow:

*Physically Handicapped.* Camp Kno-Koma (say it slowly), a free camp for diabetic children in West Virginia, has successfully adapted a program to meet the unique needs of diabetic children.[22] They are enabled to live a camp life very much like that of nonafflicted children, but one which makes the requirements of their daily regimen, such as diet, medication, and protection against insulin shock while swimming, a normal, taken-for-granted part of camp routine. The article, "Recreation Center for the Cerebral Palsied," describes a fine program for children with this illness, presently being carried on in San Francisco.[23] "Swimming for Handicapped Children" describes a swimming program carried on in Manchester, Connecticut, for youngsters suffering from polio paralysis, cerebral palsy, blindness, and muscular dystrophy.[24]

"Boys and Girls Together—Handicapped and Able Bodied," concerns a unique *Herald Tribune* "Fresh Air Fund" camp in Ridgefield, Connecticut.[25] In this camp about 30 to 40 per cent of the youngsters were seriously handicapped, but were able to get along satisfactorily in a wide variety of play activities with able-bodied children—without social or physical injuries. There are many other such examples, of an inspiring nature.

*Emotionally Maladjusted.* Here, too, there is much experimentation in terms of therapeutic play techniques. Chiefly, this consists of play sessions with very small groups of disturbed children under the guidance of an adult therapist. The experience is designed to establish trusting, friendly relationships between the individual children and the therapist, through the use of an accepting, nonrestrictive atmosphere. The child is encouraged to express himself with such projective toys as dolls and doll furniture, puppets, rubber knives and guns, clay, and other art materials. Moustakas writes: [26]

> . . . through his play the child may act out perceptions of himself, his family and others that he would not reveal in his real world. These imaginary expressions themselves may enable him to live more securely in the world of reality. Children should be given time and a place with play materials to which they can go and where they can feel free to smear and mess, to draw and paint, to create and destroy, and sometimes to recreate themselves, their families and other individuals.

He continues:

While play frequently offers emotional release to children, it is not automatically accompanied by emotional insight. The presence of an adult whose aim is to help children clarify their feelings and accept them is an important requisite and hastens the process of emotional growth.

In the conclusion of his book, Moustakas gives an encouraging account of one ordinary, unskilled parent's venture into the use of play materials with a child in a successful effort to achieve better understanding and a happier relationship.

Somewhat less common are accounts of how larger groups of disturbed children may be involved in play activities, as a therapeutic measure. One such article, "Remedial Recreation in a Child-Care Institution," describes the process of working with rejected, retarded, and poorly coordinated boys in the nine-to-twelve age range, in a home for children from broken homes, many of whom were seriously disturbed and had been involved in delinquency.[27]

## Play Activities in Camps

The chief focus of camping programs, whether we refer to part-time day camps, or full-time summer camps, should be on providing enjoyable play and living experiences that are designed to bring about the maximum favorable growth in youngsters.

In the past many traditional camps, particularly well-established private summer camps, were characterized by rigid, whistle-ruled scheduling, authoritarian leadership, and too great a stress on skill and success in competitive sports. Another unfavorable aspect of many of these camps is that too many of them were open for members of just one sex; although there might be a brother or sister camp nearby, there would be little interaction between them. As a result, play with members of the opposite sex, by its very rarity, became overexciting and therefore something to be strongly resisted or made too much of.

Many camp owners and directors have approached these problems in a thoughtful, intelligent way, and have developed the following progressive point of view.

In the well-run modern camp, there is a much less formal type of activity scheduling than in the past. Instead of authoritarian leadership, there is considerable emphasis on the role of the counselor as just that—a helpful, friendly person who offers real guidance to the children in his charge.

While sports continue to be a major part of the camp program, for the excellent values they provide, the outcomes of athletic play are carefully scrutinized, and other forms of achievement are granted prestige as well. Whenever possible, coed parties, dances, and carnivals are arranged between neighboring boys and girls camps—not on a "big dance" or "prom" level, but in a more relaxed, casual vein. A number of camps have been organized on a completely coed basis, with boys and girls sharing many activities, such as swimming, hiking, sports, dramatics, crafts, canoe trips, and eating.

More and more modern camps are taking full advantage of their country settings by placing stress on outdoor living, nature knowledge, and conservation and survival skills. This area is discussed in more detail in Chapter 12. Other camps have placed emphasis on real-life work projects (not just meaningless, artificial tasks), and on teaching such skills as driving cars, running a print shop, designing costumes, etc.

## Juvenile Delinquency

A final important aspect of the adult's relationship to childhood play has to do with juvenile delinquency. This term is a frightening one, and the public has many misconceptions about the actual extent of juvenile delinquency and the best ways of combating it.

There have been many shocking headlines about a wave of juvenile delinquency sweeping the nation. How true is this? Actually, Richard Clendenen, the Executive Director of the Senate Subcommittee Investigating Juvenile Delinquency, has pointed out that somewhat less than 5 per cent of children between the ages of ten and seventeen get into trouble with the police.[28] Not to minimize the danger, however, he has added that the number of children in trouble has increased approximately 42 per cent within the past five years, and the proportion of serious offenses seems to be rising. Obviously the problem is an important one.

In the past many authorities felt that the best solution was to provide active recreation for youngsters. This would "keep them off the streets, keep them out of trouble, and burn up their energies," and would thus solve child crime. This notion is no more a complete answer than a recently heard statement that juvenile delinquency is really adult delinquency, and the way to end it is to slap parents of erring youngsters in prison or fine them heavily.

The reason why no single, catch-all approach is valid is that juvenile delinquency is the result of many causes, including crowded, unhealthy housing conditions; broken or unhappy home settings; subnormal intelligence or personality disturbance; lack of wholesome recreational opportunities; the influence of antisocial gangs and associates; an antagonistic attitude toward adults and other authority figures; and racial and other pressures in a community tending toward conflict.

What is needed is an over-all approach, including better housing and living conditions, social workers to improve family situations, street workers to get the confidence of gangs and reshape their interests and values, psychiatric help for disturbed children, and more effective treatment centers to help those children who must be taken out of circulation.

It has already been mentioned that play is not always a successful deterrent to juvenile delinquency, because the seriously delinquent youth rarely enjoys sports activity. Team play is too confining and demanding of social discipline for him. Sheldon and Eleanor Glueck state in a report on *Delinquents in the Making* that a much higher proportion of delinquents than nondelinquents take part in such risky, adventurous activities as stealing rides and hopping trucks, smoking and drinking at an early age, running away from home, roaming streets after dark, gambling, and setting fires. "In all the major forms of exciting youthful activity afforded by the deteriorated American urban area, the delinquent as a group greatly exceeded boys who remained law abiding." [29] Many confirmed delinquent children had attended play centers and sports programs (often they were directed there by police or probation officers), but they failed to stick, and soon found more excitement in vacant lots, railroad yards, poolrooms, dance halls, and penny arcades.

What can be done about it? The Gluecks suggest: [29a]

. . . settlement houses, school-community centers, church centers, boys clubs and other agencies must take into account the preferences of these adventure-thirsty boys who dislike intensive supervision and tend to turn to delinquency as a congenial way of life. Such agencies should experiment with various means of attracting and guiding youngsters of this type into at least socially harmless, if not positively constructive, channels.

In all fairness, it should be pointed out that while sports and other forms of organized play may not appeal to children with serious delinquent tendencies, they certainly do a great deal for children of fairly stable homes and backgrounds who grow up in, or close to, slum areas. For them, the constructive values and healthy enjoyment of challenging play represent a driving force for good social adjustment—an important weight on the scales that decide what the child's life is to be like.

A final point is that, although juvenile crime is usually dramatically publicized, with banner headlines and jarring photographs, constructive efforts to deter it are seldom given the same amount of public attention. This is understandable, for combating delinquency is not exciting or spectacular work. It is a matter of slow, methodical, day-by-day laboring on many fronts, of minor gains, of the gradually won confidence of a single child, and of the changing code of behavior of a neighborhood gang. It demands community realization that this is everybody's job—for when the trigger of a zip-gun is squeezed, everybody suffers. All adults, whether they are parents, teachers, club leaders, or social workers, have a stake in this problem, and all must contribute their best efforts, for the sake of their own families, communities, and nation.

## *Summary*

This chapter outlines the circumstances under which adults may logically become involved in the leadership and guidance of children's play activities. It describes what their contributions may consist of, and lists five types of settings or sponsors for organized play: schools, community centers and youth organizations, the home, treatment centers for handicapped children, and camps. The closing discussion deals with juvenile delinquency and the relation of play activities to its prevention and treatment.

# CHAPTER 4

# EFFECTIVE
# GROUP LEADERSHIP

This chapter is concerned with the role of the adult leader who is working with groups of children in play situations. It does not attempt to deal with the many informal, short-lived groups which youngsters form or join for play purposes; such groups rarely have regular meeting places or times and often resist adult "interference." Instead, it has to do with the type of club or group which meets more or less regularly, in a designated place, with the assistance of adult supervision or direction. Many children who are as young as seven or eight belong to such groups, which may be sponsored by the Boy or Girl Scouts, Camp Fire Girls, community centers, settlement houses, public recreation agencies and playgrounds, and religious organizations.

To understand properly how the leader may function most effectively, it is necessary to know something about how groups operate—and the important part the group experience may have on the developing personalities of the participants. To some, any discussion of group dynamics may seem farfetched and unnecessary. Such individuals may josh: "Children get together and play. They always have and always will. That's all there is to it; you're making a big thing out of nothing. Why all this concern about what goes on in the group?"

The answer to such queries is short and to the point.

Perhaps the most important outcome of group play is healthy socialization for each child who takes part in it. This does not occur automatically. For some children, group play can be a positive, happy, inviting, and encouraging experience. For others, it may be negative, frustrating, and uninviting.

30

Grace Coyle has written: [30]

I believe that groups . . . if properly understood and sympathetically led, can provide for the participants a kind of social nourishment which will enhance life and encourage growth. If a group, through the interaction of the members and the guidance of the leader, is friendly, warm and accepting, it can give to its members a chance to experience mutual relationships and the diffused but significant securities that come from the sense of belonging. For different individuals, and at different age levels, this kind of acceptance will have varied meanings. For many it can contribute to emotional stability and security and can give acceptable guidance to both positive and negative feelings.

How can an adult leader tell what is happening to the children in a group? It is not always easy, for a basic fact about the group process is that things are happening on two levels. On one level, which might be called the surface, children play games, carry on arts and crafts, and engage in other activities. On another, less obvious plane, they are expressing aggressions, frustrations, and feelings of hostility or friendship and, in many minute incidents and experiences, making a contribution to the group life and reacting to the acts of others.

What sort of specific questions may the leader ask to get at this subsurface, or undercurrent aspect of group life? Here are some:

## Looking at Groups

*Membership.* Who makes up the group? What are the members like? How old are they? What sex? What sort of homes and neighborhoods do they seem to come from? How many are there in the group?

*Reasons for Joining.* Why have the children gotten together in this group? Is it because they have similar play interests? Have they been drawn together from different neighborhoods and backgrounds by some community-wide or national youth-serving organization? Is it primarily a neighborhood friendship group?

*Common Needs.* Perhaps they share certain pressing, common needs; it is very likely that this is so. What are these needs? Have the children expressed them themselves, or are they not clear? How do they jibe with the goals and purposes of the leader, the sponsoring agency, and the community?

*Group Relationships.* What kind of interpersonal relationships exist in the group? How do the individual members feel about each other? Are there cliques or subgroups? How do the sexes get along together? What seems to determine popularity or unpopularity? Do some children seem to be rejected and left out of things? Why? What is group membership based on? Are there formal criteria for accepting some members—and turning away others who do not measure up?

*Activity Choices.* What are the most popular, accepted program activities? Do all participants seem to enjoy these fully? Have other materials been tried?

*Inner Leadership.* How is the program of the group actually decided on and carried out? To what extent do the children themselves participate in this planning? How are conflicts and disputes resolved, and how are problems met? How are special ventures and projects evaluated, and what kinds of social outcomes and learnings are voiced and discussed openly by the group members?

*Outcomes.* In the long run, what sort of common bonds, loyalties and mutual interests seem to be developing in the group?

Certainly, few recreation leaders would attempt to "score" a group mathematically on the basis of these questions. They are simply intended to provide a point of view, a stimulus to help one look at a group as it develops, with broadened and deepened perceptions.

## The Group and the Leader

When a group of children first gets together, they are likely to be a collection of more or less self-centered individualists. Quite naturally, each child will be most aware of his own needs, impulses, and concerns, and will not have developed attitudes or behavior patterns which place great emphasis on the group's welfare. It is also very likely, however, that, because of his similar age and background and the fact that he has voluntarily joined together with the others, he shares certain common personal needs and potential play interests with them. It is up to the leader to discover and satisfy these needs and interests, to awaken group awareness and loyalty, and to encourage children to develop healthy, effective techniques of group action.

What leadership approaches are most likely to bring this about?

*Types of Leadership.* Within recent years three chief types of group leadership have been described and explored in experimental settings. These include: (1) authoritarian, or dictatorial; (2) permissive, or laissez-faire; (3) and democratic, in which the emphasis is on mutuality of planning and decision-making between the leader and group members. Ruth Cunningham has expanded these types into five categories, with particular reference to teachers: [31]

1. Complete adult rule and child obedience.
2. Planless, catch-as-catch-can relationship, with no attempt to control or organize the situation effectively.
3. Teacher planning with individual group members. Here there is some communication of ideas and joint planning between the teacher and children, with resultant growth of understanding and initiative on the part of the children. However, there is little group interaction.
4. Adult-directed group planning. Children may do their own planning under adult supervision and direction. They do not establish their own rules or boundaries.
5. The group manages itself through truly democratic group planning. This is the most desirable approach and, obviously, the most difficult to achieve.

Cunningham points out that a good teacher is likely to make use of any or all of these approaches, depending on the factors of the particular situation and the previous experiences of the children, but that, ideally, the aim would be to achieve (4) and (5). One factor is the age of the children; youngsters of seven or eight are not likely to be able to take on too much responsibility, while those of eleven or twelve may be much more capable. It also depends on the size of the group. Most authorities agree that the ideal number of participants for the group process to operate effectively is close to ten or twelve. Practically speaking, some leaders will have groups numbering up to forty, fifty, or even in the hundreds. With a small group, there is likely to be a much more personal, close relationship between the adult leader and the children, resulting in a real "we" feeling and a truly democratic atmosphere. On the other hand, with very large groups, the leader will often have to operate in an authoritarian way; while he may welcome suggestions and reactions of individual children, it will be necessary for him to take on much more authority and maintain a tight degree of control. When a leader is faced with a group numbering, possibly, in the hundreds, it is desirable for him to introduce the kinds of activity that put children into smaller, face-to-face groups (games, team sports, informal dramatics, crafts projects, etc.) so they can build social relationships, even without the direct guidance or help of an adult leader.

Even when other factors are right, the ability of children to govern themselves in a play group does not come automatically. Cunningham offers caution: [32]

> Freedom may be frustrating to an individual or group if no security is provided. It is evident that certain skills are needed if an advanced pattern of self-management is to be attained. If the freedom is provided before the appropriate skills have been learned, there is little likelihood that other than a chaotic situation will result. Frustration due to lack of security will lead, almost without exception, to aggression or withdrawal. . . . During the learning of these skills of interaction, it may be necessary for an adult to direct the learning and to choose areas in which the skills are to be practiced.

What are the broad stages of a play group's development, and what role does the adult leader play in each of these? No two situations are the same, of course, and the sequence is likely to be affected by the physical setting and available equipment and materials. However, here is a general description of what is likely to occur:

## Stages of Group Development

The leader meets with the children and begins to get acquainted with them, unless, as in the case of a schoolteacher or parent, they already know each other quite well. He may interest them in briefly mastered activities, such as simple projects, games, and stunts. Through these, they begin to gain confidence in the situation and in him as a leader, as well as enjoyment from the activities. Singing and dancing, active and quiet games, and dramatics may all be used on a simple level at this early stage, although it may be wise also to rely on some activities which children can attack by themselves, such as crafts projects, puzzles, or physical activity apparatus.

At an early stage the leader and the children should talk about the sort of play activities they enjoy the most, and how they like them carried on. The leader may ask some of the youngsters who have ideas that are new to the others whether they would lead activities, or, possibly, bring needed equipment or tools from home. He may also introduce new activities himself before too long. All such program materials should, at this stage, allow for full participation of all the group members and for fairly sure success and easy enjoyment. There should be considerable interplay among the children, with no rigid teams or "sides" being formed and with no continuing opportunity for one child to be "starred" or others frustrated or discouraged.

Gradually, as the club continues to meet, the leader encourages group thinking and discussion. Each child speaks out more freely about what he enjoys doing, the choices he wishes to make, and aspects of the group that he likes or dislikes. Through such exchanges of ideas the youngsters are helped to recognize and understand their own needs, desires, abilities, and limitations. They see the necessity for certain kinds of behavior and for group cooperation.

At all times the leader must try to be sensitive to the total group climate, which should be friendly, relaxed, and accepting. Simultaneously he should be aware of the individuals in the group. In any new setting certain faces and personalities will stand out first in the leader's mind. One child will be extremely aggressive or pugnacious. Another will be very trusting and friendly. One will have flaming red hair and freckles; another will have buckteeth. Many of the children, simply because they have no outstanding or striking traits, will remain for a while almost faceless or nameless for the leader.

Gradually, however, each child will take on an individual identity in the leader's mind. He will recognize that there is a social scale among the children, ranging from the most highly accepted and desired to those who are barely tolerated or even disliked and rejected. This scale of popularity is not haphazardly established; the leader will find that the best-liked children are those who show initiative, have well-rounded personality traits, and usually are skilled in the sorts of activity that the group values highly.

At the same time that he recognizes and encourages these "solid citizens," the adult leader is likely to recognize those children who have poor status—who do not function well in the group. They are all too easy to find; they do not have close friends; they are ineffective in play activities; they are likely to spend much of their time daydreaming and isolated from the group; in appearance, they may be sloppy and untidy; often they will be subject to outspoken hostility or ridicule from the other group members. Some children may profess to be socially disinterested because of solitary concerns and hobbies; the leader may respect this pose but should realize that it is likely to be a shield covering up lack of confidence in the group setting. Other socially ineffective children, instead of withdrawing, may force themselves on the others, trying to gain esteem by being noisy, aggressive, and boastful. Here too, beneath surface assurance, lies shyness and insecurity.

As much as possible, the leader should try to help such children find security and acceptance in the group. However, he should realize that children are not all capable of making a good adjustment to a group. Their personal problems may be such that it is not possible to spare them the insults, conflicts, and disappointments that often come as part of the rough-and-tumble of group life but that, for them, assume the dimension of traumatic experiences. If they cannot function at all in the group, and if they are serving to disrupt and distract the others to no good purpose, the leader may decide that his chief function is recreation, not therapy. Therefore, it may be necessary for him to refer them to a skilled therapist or a more protected play setting after a conference of the adults involved in the problem.

In time, the leader may strive to broaden the recreational horizons of the children by suggesting or encouraging special events, projects, parties, tournaments, shows, trips, and visits. These require a high degree of group self-discipline, realistic planning, and cooperation and, because of their special nature, are greatly enjoyed by youngsters. Particularly if their interest seems to be at a low ebb, such events keep group spirit high.

Gradually, as group members develop strong allegiances to each other and to their joint alliance, and as they achieve efficiency in terms of functioning independently, the leader may permit his influence to diminish greatly. While young children are likely to continue to depend on the leader, older ones may take on major responsibility for organizing activities, recruiting and governing membership, maintaining discipline, and planning special events.

A final, important task of the adult leader throughout this entire process is to interpret the feelings of the outside community to the children, helping them understand why grownups feel and act as they do, and why ideas and plans that the children have may meet certain reactions—favorable or unfavorable—in the adult world. In turn, he represents the children in their relations with outsiders and community forces. This is particularly true of the relationship between "gang" youths and "street" social workers, but every group of children engaging in organized play in a community depends to some degree on their adult leader for this sort of help.

## The Leader and the Children

As much as possible, the leader should have a personal interest in each youngster in the group. This means knowing a great deal about him—his family and home background and his individual problems, interests, triumphs, and failures. It means showing warmth and sympathy toward him, talking with him often on a person-to-person basis, and, if at all practicable, visiting him at home or taking part in other activities with him and his friends away from the recreation center. This concern of the leader should be fairly distributed among all the children in a play group; some youngsters may seek to monopolize it, but he should not permit this to happen.

The leader must earn and justify the liking and respect of the children as an adult—not just as "one of the gang." While he wants them to feel at ease with him, they also have a need to look up to and admire a friendly adult who represents the grown-up world to them in its best form. One social worker made a practice of shooting dice for money with boys in a neighborhood gang, in an effort to get them to accept him fully. He soon realized that he had made a mistake; while they felt that it was all right for them to gamble, they knew that it was not approved of by society, and he lost considerable status in their eyes by doing it. They felt that as their leader he should have set an example for them.

At all times the leader should treat the children as responsible, capable individuals who are worthy of trust and confidence—unless they show by consistent misbehavior that they cannot accept this role. They should not be "talked-down-to" condescendingly, although it may be necessary to simplify ideas and information in discussions with them when certain concepts are too complicated for them to grasp readily.

The leader should try to encourage and give praise whenever possible. This policy should not be so extended that praise becomes meaningless; when children have failed or done poorly, they should be made aware of the goals that have not been attained. The leader should always avoid excessive sarcasm, harshness, ridicule, or obvious strong emotion.

When antisocial behavior appears, he should not be shocked excessively by it, but should make an effort to understand and minimize it and to provide more socially acceptable forms of expression or gratification. No matter what form it takes—fighting, lying, or stealing—this sort of behavior should be viewed as a symptom of a child's need. One classroom teacher had a boy who came to school on certain days ready to fight at the drop of a hat. Usually he was in an unmanageable temper tantrum before half the morning had passed. On other days he was quiet and cooperative. Eventually the teacher found out that the youngster's parents sometimes fought bitterly. The boy's "bad" days invariably came as a result of his parents' having quarreled earlier in the morning. There was no easy solution to this problem, but it gives one an idea of the pressures operating on children and makes one less likely to have rigid expectations of what childhood behavior should be like. Even the worst problem youngsters can be understood, reached, and helped—unless they are so emotionally disturbed that they simply cannot fit into a typical play group.

A final essential attitude on the part of the leader is a conviction that he is involved in a vitally important task—which he is. Helping young children in the development of their personalities and the achievement of a happier life is rarely dramatic or glamorous work, but its rewards, in terms of human satisfactions, can be great.

## How to Present Activities

Much of the foregoing material has been theoretical, rather than immediately practical. In the latter sphere, just how does a leader set about presenting a game, a dance, a song, a crafts project, or a dramatic skit? Is there any infallible, set procedure, or is it up to the leader to use whatever teaching method occurs to him on the spot? How does the leader select activities? How are parties or "fun sessions" programmed? Where can the leader get help in solving these problems?

Here are some down-to-earth suggestions regarding the leadership of various kinds of play activities.

*Self-Preparation.* Whatever the activity, the leader should be familiar with it himself before attempting to lead it. If necessary, he may get the help or the advice of a capable specialist or resource person or attend a course in recreation leadership offered by a nearby school, college, or social agency. A group of parents living in the same neighborhood may join together for special classes in a particular skill with the aid of a trained leader; Scout mothers often do this. The unskilled leader will also find much help in his local library; there are many books, pamphlets, phonograph records, and instructional kits having to do with various phases of recreation leadership.

*Needed Equipment.* Before any play activity begins, the leader should be certain that all needed equipment, tools, and materials are on hand, clean, and in good condition. Children may often volunteer to help with this responsibility; they enjoy it and must do their best to live up to it.

*Arouse Interest.* When an activity is to be presented for the first time, the leader should stimulate interest in it and give the participants some idea of what lies ahead. He may tell an anecdote about it, show some finished products (as in crafts work), take the children to an exhibition or game, show a film or photographs in advance, or hear about the experiences of some of the children who have already participated in the activity. This should be done quickly and in a lively way.

*Take Formation.* If the activity requires that the players take partners or teams or stand in a special formation, as in a game or dance, it may be best for them to do this before the actual instruction. Thus, demonstration will have immediate meaning for them, and they will be able to go right into the activity when it has been shown, rather than necessitate delay and confusion in getting reorganized for it.

*Demonstrate and Do.* The most direct and effective way to teach most recreational activities is through physical demonstration. This is not because the leader wants the children to copy him exactly, but because they learn best by seeing it actually done. He may show a stunt or other action himself or ask children who are already familiar with it to show it. Without any delay for verbal descriptions, all the children should then practice it as quickly as possible.

In the case of most games and dances, the leader should divide the activity into logical, meaningful sections; there might be three sections to a dance, each involving a major action and set to a different part of the music. After each section is shown, the children would be "walked through" that action. When the entire activity has been shown and practiced in these major sections, the leader might sum it up, relating the separate parts to each other. Then it would be done as a complete unit. This method of instruction may not appeal to those who think in terms of teaching the "whole" activity, but in the case of any game or dance or song which is at all long or involved, it is the most practical.

*Teaching Emphases.* The leader should work enthusiastically and with drive. If the group is small, he may be personal and fairly subdued in his approach. If it is large, he should raise his voice, exaggerate his movements, and make sure that he is stationed where he can easily be seen and heard by all participants. The leader should not focus all his attention on one or two youngsters, but should be sure to shift his position and gaze so that he is close to, and directs his voice right at, different sections of the group from time to time. In leading singing, for instance, it would be a mistake for the leader to confine his gaze, gestures, and directions to the people immediately in front of him; he must give *all* the participants the feeling that he is leading *them,* even if they are sitting far to his side. As much as possible, the leader should avoid a "do this" approach and should stress a "let's" attitude. Whenever he can, he should involve himself in the activity along with the youngsters unless he is needed to supervise it in some other way.

In his teaching, the leader should realize that it is important for children fully to understand the total enterprise or activity and to have some grasp of what the product or outcomes may be. This insight should be given at the start, long before all the minute rules, playing strategy, and techniques are shown. If insight is given soon enough about the general nature of the activity, errors, mistakes, and problems may be dealt with as it is played— always in an encouraging, easygoing, and friendly way.

*Play It.* Once sufficient understanding has been gained to begin the activity, it should be played. Occasionally it may be interrupted briefly for more pointers to be given; the leader should also recognize that the children themselves will help each other with suggestions, commands, and actual physical aid. There is always much of this impromptu learning and leadership within any group. The activity should be enjoyed as long as it is real fun and should then be ended. The children might give their reactions to it and offer suggestions as to how it might be done again with greater enjoyment or how rules might be changed to be more effective.

*Play It Again.* If the activity has been well chosen and presented, the children will probably want to play it again and again.

This list of suggestions applies chiefly to those activities which may be learned and participated in in a single session, rather than to those which develop gradually over a period of time, such as a dramatics presentation, or a crafts or hobby project. However, the basic points given here about self-preparation, arousing interest, teaching in logical sections of activity, teaching through demonstration, giving insight, and encouraging inner leadership within the group apply to all sorts of play activities in greater or lesser degrees.

## Programming Play Sessions

In planning any single session, whether it be a regular meeting of a club or a special party, activities must be chosen which are suited to the age, numbers, and previous recreation experiences of the children. Many children tend to want to stay with familiar and well-liked activities and may protest vocally against new kinds of program stunts. However, the leader should not hesitate to push beyond the tried-and-true if he feels the group would enjoy and profit from new kinds of experiences.

When planning a single meeting remember that the leader should be there early, or ahead of the scheduled meeting time, to welcome early-comers. If members of the group have agreed to take on leadership tasks for a special party, they may also come early to put up decorations or prepare refreshments. If the children are slow in coming in, some sort of free play or self-absorbed activities, such as table games, may be provided for those who arrive on time.

During the course of the play session there should be a variety of kinds of activities. Some should be quite familiar and require no instruction or review at all. Others may be new and will challenge and interest the participants because of this. Activities should be concerned with a variety of interests and skills, so that all group members, no matter what their special abilities and talents, may gain some degree of success and satisfaction. The youngster who reads a great deal may prefer a quiz game. The less verbal child who is physically well-coordinated may excel at games or dancing. The child who has neither studious interests nor athletic prowess but has a good sense of design may prefer arts and crafts. Each child in a truly varied program has the chance to "shine" and to help others or assume momentary leadership.

In terms of the nature of activities, some may bring immediate enjoyment, while others may be slanted toward long-term goals. Some are individual-centered; others require intensive group interplay. Some involve the leader's direction; others give complete release to the group. Some demand strenuous action; others are quite restful. Some involve fierce competition; others are strongly cooperative in nature. In any session, or in any continued series of play sessions, there should be a good balance of activities. In any session there should be some time for free play or even nonparticipation. Children should not all be expected to enjoy every activity.

A reasonable amount of time should be allowed at the end of each session to clean up, chat, and discuss future plans and projects. Informal evaluation of this sort is always desirable.

## Summary

In this chapter the major emphasis is placed on the adult leader's role in meeting with and guiding groups of children in play activities. Aspects of children's groups are described, together with several different approaches toward leadership. In a more immediately practical vein, several teaching guides for presenting activities are offered, accompanied by brief suggestions for programming play sessions.

# PART TWO

# A WORLD
# OF
# PLAY ACTIVITIES

# CHAPTER 5

# ACTIVE GAMES
# AND CONTESTS

Among the most popular and useful play materials for children in the six-to-twelve age range are active games, stunts, contests, and relays. These vigorous and enjoyable activities provide physical release, improve social growth, and help children learn and improve many important bodily skills. For youngsters up to the age of eight or nine, games should be quite simple. Following this age, they enjoy playing more complicated games and are increasingly able to subordinate their own impulses and desires to the needs of their group or team. It is in this setting that children learn about fair play and sportsmanship, the acceptance of responsibility, the ability to take victory or defeat in good grace, and obedience to necessary rules.

## Guides for Game Leadership

Before beginning any game session, the leader should be certain that all needed equipment or materials are available and in good condition. Responsibility for this may be given to children in the group, who should also play a part in planning the session as much as possible.

The leader's attitude and enthusiasm help to put each game across; he should therefore present only games or stunts that he believes in strongly and is sure the group will enjoy. Such games will be neither too simple nor too complex for the age level involved. They should be suitable for the numbers involved and the space where the activity will be carried on. They should allow for maximum participation and for rotation of child leadership or starring roles. They should also be thoroughly familiar to the leader; if he is to have confidence, he must be sure of the rules and playing procedures.

When teaching, the leader should expect full attention. The atmosphere should not be repressive or drill-like, but the children should understand that this is a time when full cooperation is needed and wild horseplay is out of place.

During the actual instruction the leader should give a demonstration of the game, rather than describe it verbally. This should be brief and to the point and should be done *after* the group has taken the needed formation or position.

When showing the game, the leader should stand where he can be seen and heard by all the participants. When teaching, he should anticipate possible difficulties and trouble spots and try to clear them up in advance.

As soon as the activity has been demonstrated, it should be played. If minor problems or questions arise, they can be settled while the game is going on. If there is real confusion and uncertainty, the leader should stop the action, clear up the problem, and resume the game.

Rules are meant to add to the fun of the game—but not to be so rigid or all-important that they take away from the pleasure involved. Essential rules should be explained and clearly understood and should then be obeyed at all times. If the leader's enforcement and decisions are alert and fair, the children will have confidence in them and will not try to cheat on the rules or to argue against their application.

A game should continue as long as enthusiasm is high. When it begins to lag, the game should be stopped and a new game introduced.

In any single game session the leader should develop a plan in advance which allows for a good variety of activities, as was described in Chapter 3. This plan should be flexible enough to permit changes on the spot. Among other qualities, it should alternate strenuous with quiet activities. This safeguard, plus the fact that children are given a chance to relax physically while they are forming new teams or learning new games, usually gives them sufficient rest during any game session, so that special time need not be given to "time-out" breaks.

This chapter presents the following types of activities: tag and chase games, relays, ball games, and self-testing and stunt events. In each grouping they are presented in approximate order of difficulty, from simple to complex. Suggestions as to the recommended size of group and type of play area are included.

## TAG AND CHASE GAMES

Most of these games can be played with groups of children numbering between six and approximately twenty-five in fairly limited indoor or outdoor play areas. A few require additional space or numbers; they will be so described.

**Exchange Tag.** Children sit in chairs or, if space permits, stand in a circle. One child is selected to be *It*. He stands in the center. The leader calls out the names of two children in the circle (if they do not all know each other's names, he may give them all numbers, and then call out two numbers). These two run to exchange seats or places in the circle before *It* can tag them. If a runner is tagged, he becomes *It* and the old *It* takes his place in the circle. If no player is tagged before reaching the other player's spot, the leader calls out two new names or numbers.

In guiding this game, the leader should be sure that the names of all the youngsters are called and that no child is permitted to remain *It* too long.

**Come Along.** Players sit in a circle of chairs or stand in a circle facing in, shoulder to shoulder. *It* skips around the inside of the circle. He takes another child by the hand, saying, "Come along." They skip along together, and the second child takes another by the hand, saying, "Come along." This is continued until a signal, "Run for it!" is given by the leader or the first player. All the players who were holding hands run for the empty positions. The one who is left without a seat or place to stand is *It* as the game is played again.

**Shadow Tag.** Children scatter about a play area, preferably outdoors, since there should be a strong enough overhead light for each player to have a fairly distinct shadow. One player is chosen as *It*. To catch another player, *It* must step on his shadow. When he has done this, that player becomes *It*. If *It* calls out "Shadows cross!" the other players must all run across to the opposite side of the play area, which gives him a better change to catch one of them.

**Stoop Tag.** Children scatter. One player is chosen as *It*. He can tag any player who is not in a stooped position. If he does this, that person becomes *It* and tries to tag another. If children stay in a stooped position too long, so *It* does not have a chance to tag them, he may stand back a few feet from any player and count to three. That player must stand up and run before he has finished counting or he becomes *It*.

**Hindu Tag.** This is like Stoop Tag. Players are immune from being tagged by *It* if they take a position on their knees with their foreheads touching the ground.

**Tree Tag.** This is like the previous games. Any player touching a tree is safe from being tagged by *It*. One way to play it is to have players call out the number of times they have touched a tree; when they have gone to it three times, they may no longer return to it for safety.

**Iron Tag.** This is similar to Tree Tag. Any person touching an iron object or structure is safe from being tagged. It might seem to adults that children, in playing tag games, would tend to stick close to objects that give them immunity. Actually they do not. They love to tempt fate, and will usually leave the safety spot to run past *It* and risk getting caught.

**Slap Jack.** Players stand in a single circle with hands behind their backs. *It* runs around the outside of the circle; he slaps the hands of a player in the circle as he goes. This player runs in the opposite direction around the outside, trying to get back to the empty spot before *It*. The first child to return to the spot stands in it; the other becomes *It* and goes around the outside.

This game may also be played in couples, with one couple going around the outside and other couples standing in the circle (each person holding a partner's hand). The action may be varied so they must walk or hop around the outside. In limited space this is a safer way to play the game.

**Moving Day.** This game is played in the classroom. If seats are movable, they should be placed in rows (one behind the other). If they are fixed, they will probably already be in rows. Empty seats should be put in a corner, or if they are not movable, should have a book put on them so they will not be used. Between each two rows an *It* (known as the renter) walks up and down. As he moves along the "street," homeowners behind or in front of him quickly cross over, exchanging homes. The Renter tries to move into one of the vacant houses whenever this happens. If he is successful, the displaced homeowner becomes the new Renter and walks up and down between the rows.

To add interest the leader may call out, "It's Moving Day!" Then every homeowner in the room must find a new home in a different part of town. (He may not take a seat in the row he was just in.) This gives the Renter better chance to find a home if he has been having difficulty.

**Link Tag.** One player is *It* as the others scatter about a play space with clearly marked borders. *It* tags another player, who joins hands with him. They tag another player, who joins the line. They continue to chase and tag other players. (Only the two players at the end of the line may do the actual tagging.) Players who cross the boundary lines have broken the rules and must join the line. The game goes on until a certain number of players have been caught or until a period of time has gone by. Then one of the players who was *not* caught becomes *It*.

If there are enough players and play space, the game may be played with two *Its,* who compete to see whose line can catch the most within a set period of time. (If a line is broken at any time, it must be joined again before it can tag other players.)

**Triplet Tag.** Children join hands in groups of three and scatter about the play space. One group is given a piece of red or white cloth; this group is *It*. *It* tries to tag another group, keeping hands joined at all times. When a group is tagged, it is given the cloth, becomes *It,* and tries to tag another group. If a group is tagged three times, it may be eliminated from the game.

**Red Light.** This is a popular old street game, which may also be played on a playground or in a gymnasium. One person is chosen to be *It*. He stands on a home base line. The other children all stand on a line at least 25 feet behind him. (His back is to them.) *It* closes his eyes, counts to ten, shouts, "Red Light," and turns about quickly. While he is counting, the other players run toward him. When they hear him call, "Red Light," they must stop dead in their tracks, for if he sees them moving when he turns to face them, they must return to the starting line. The game is repeated until one child gets close enough to tap *It* on the back while he is counting. He then turns and chases them back to the starting line. The first player he tags becomes *It,* and the game is begun again.

**Bronco Tag** (Diagram 1). Players scatter in groups of two. One child is the front end, or Head, of the Bronco, and the other, with his hands clasped around his partner's waist, is the Tail. In addition, one child becomes a Chaser, and another a Runner. The Chaser pursues the Runner. The Runner, to avoid getting caught, tries to get his arms around the Tail of any Bronco in the game. If he does this, he becomes the new Tail, and the child who had been the Head now becomes a Runner. If the Runner is caught before he can catch and join a Bronco, he reverses roles with

**Diagram 1**

the Chaser and pursues him. As the game is played, each Bronco may dodge and twist about to avoid the Runner but may not use arms to push him off.

**Cat and Rat.** The players stand in a circle, about two feet apart, facing toward the center. One player becomes the Cat, and another the Rat. They stand on opposite sides of the circle; at a signal the Cat chases the Rat. The Rat may run between any of the openings between the players in the circle, but they must then immediately join hands, thus closing the hole. The Cat may run through these joined openings; the Rat may not. Thus, as he flees, the Rat gradually closes up all the holes until it is easy for the Cat to catch him. When he is caught, the Cat and Rat either reverse roles or choose two new players to continue the game.

In another version of this, known as "Sewing up the Gaps," the Rat is permitted to run through the closed openings but the Cat is not. The object of the game is for the Rat to "close up all the gaps" before the Cat can catch him.

**Have You Seen My Sheep?** All the players but one stand in a circle, facing in. *It* walks around the outside. Touching any child on the shoulder, he asks, "Have you seen my sheep?" The child who is touched replies, "What was he wearing?" *It* describes the clothing of any one of the other players in the game. As soon as the child who was touched guesses the right one, he calls his name out and chases him around the outside of the circle, trying to catch him before he can get back to his place. *It* does not run, but steps into the empty spot in the circle. If the chaser catches the one whose clothing was described, that child becomes *It*. If not, the chaser becomes *It*.

**Bears and Cattle.** Two base lines, parallel to each other and about fifty feet apart, are marked off. A Bear Cave is placed at the side of the play area at an equal distance from the two base lines. All the players but one become Cattle and stand in two equal groups behind the base lines. One child, the Bear, stands in the Cave area. The Bear growls, as a signal, and the Cattle all run across toward each other's base line. The Bear runs out and tags as many Cattle as possible. The tagged Cattle become Bears and go to the Cave. They join hands with the first Bear, in a line; the first of the Cattle caught always is placed at the other end of the line. The game continues with the Bear line growling and then rushing out to tag as many Cattle as possible as they cross over. The two end Bears are the only ones who are allowed to tag. If the Bear line breaks, it must reunite before new Cattle may be tagged. The last of the Cattle to be caught becomes the beginning Bear when the game is played again.

**Forest Lookout.** Two concentric circles of children are formed. The outside circle members are Fire-fighters. Those in the inner circle are Trees. One player, the Lookout, stands in the center. He calls out loudly, "Fire in the mountain, RUN, RUN, RUN!" When they hear the last "RUN!" the Fire-fighters run around the outside of the circle to the right. After a few moments, the Lookout quietly moves in front of one of the standing Trees. When the Fire-fighters see him do this, they hurry to do the same. The Fire-fighter who cannot find a Tree becomes a Lookout and goes into the center. Each time the game is repeated, the Trees and Fire-fighters change places with each other, so everyone gets a chance to run. From time to time the children should be asked to step backward, since the circle tends to grow smaller.

**Crows and Cranes.** This game is suitable for as many as fifty or seventy players and requires a large play area. A center line is drawn across the area. A safety line is then marked on either side of the center line, approximately forty feet away, so there is a distance of about eighty feet between the safety lines. The players are divided into two equal teams. They stand on opposite sides of the center line. The lines face each other and are about six feet apart. One team is called Crows and the other Cranes. The leader, standing at the end of the center line, calls out a signal. If he calls, "Crows!" the Crows run toward their safety line, trying to reach it before the Cranes can tag them. If he calls, "Cranes!" the Cranes run, and the Crows pursue.

If he calls, "Crawfish!" no one runs. To heighten interest and promote false starts, the leader may deliberately draw out the beginning of the word with a "c-r-r" sound, so the players will not know what is coming.

Each team receives a point for every member of the opposite team tagged before reaching the safety line. It loses a point for every one of its own players running in the wrong direction, running on the "Crawfish" call, or failing to run on a call. The team with the most points after a set period of time wins.

### RELAYS

Another popular and useful type of game is the relay, in which the participants are divided into teams of equal size, which then race, one player at a time, to complete some action or stunt. These are particularly suitable, because all children have a chance to participate, without any great pressure being exerted on individuals. Considerable team spirit is usually aroused, but it takes a cooperative form, with each player rooting and working for his own team. Children enjoy relays especially because many of them are humorous or physically challenging. As a rule those which involve "silly" stunts and small movements are more suitable to indoor or party events. Other relays which demand more physical exertion are usually best played in a gymnasium or on an outdoor playfield.

GUIDES FOR LEADING RELAYS

When presenting a relay, explain it quickly and then have the first player of each team try it. This first player may also be appointed as a leader for his team to make sure they understand the rules and will abide by them. Children may pick their own team leader. A suitable number of children on each team may be about six or seven. If there is an uneven number, one player on the team that is short may run again.

Children should be given a distinct signal to begin the relay. There should also be a definite way for a team to show that they have completed the action. (They raise hands or sit down.) There should be no question as to which team won.

In scoring, points may be given for the first, second, and third teams to finish, such as "five for first, three for second, and one for third." Children may enjoy giving their team a name, such as that of a favorite college, football or baseball team, or color.

As a rule girls may participate in these activities fairly equally with boys, particularly in the partylike stunts which place a premium on dexterity and balance. In the rough-and-tumble relays boys are likely to be somewhat more successful, not always because they are physically superior, but because they enjoy this sort of play more than girls.

Keep safety in mind at all times in relays, as a fairly high pitch of excitement may be aroused. If the games are being played indoors, make sure that there is no furniture or other dangerous obstruction from which children may receive injuries.

There may be different procedures for different relays, but the following rules usually apply: When approaching a turning line, a player must cross the line with both feet before turning to come back to place. When he approaches his own team, he must cross the starting line or directly touch the next player before that child can begin. If he is bringing a ball or other equipment back, he must *give* it to the next player, not *throw* it to him. Usually when a player has completed his turn, he goes directly to the rear of his line and waits there.

**Hobble Relay** (Diagram 2). Teams are in single file behind a starting line. The first player in each team lifts his left knee to his chest and holds

Diagram 2

his left foot with his right hand. On his right foot, he hops forward to the turning line (25 or 30 feet is a good distance). He changes position there and hops back on his left foot to touch off the next player in line.

**Crooked-walk Relay.** The first player on each team steps forward on his right foot and crosses his left foot behind it, moving as far forward as he can before placing his weight on the left foot. He then crosses his right foot behind his left and continues moving forward in this "crooked walk" way until he reaches a turning line. He may then either return the same way or run back to his line to touch off the second player. The method of returning should be decided in advance by the leader and children.

**Triple-squat Relay.** Team members squat in lines, one behind the other, about two feet apart. The first player in each team rises and runs completely around his line, starting to the right and traveling clockwise. When he returns, he bends his knees and does three squats in quick succession. Then the next player goes through the same action, and each following player in turn.

Diagram 3

**Kangaroo Relay** (Diagram 3). Teams of equal size line up in file formation. The first player holds a large ball such as a volleyball or rubber playground ball. If one of these is not available, a large beanbag, block of wood, balloon, or even a knotted towel may be used. At a signal, the beginning player places the ball between his knees and runs (or jumps) forward toward the turning line. He may not use his hands to hold the ball in place. If he drops the ball, he must pick it up, replace it between his knees at the point where it fell, and start to move again. After crossing the turning line with both feet, the first player may hold the ball in his hands and run back to his line to touch off the next player.

**Over-and-Under Relay.** Teams of equal size stand in single file. To begin, each first player is holding a fairly large ball; he passes this ball over his head to the player behind him. This player passes the ball between his legs to the player behind him. This is continued, alternating over and under, until the ball reaches the last player, who runs with it to the front and starts passing it back again. The game continues as in all relays until all the players have completed the action and the first player is back in his place again.

This game may be modified so the ball is passed directly back over all the players' heads; it is then called "Archball."

**Wheelbarrow Relay** (Diagram 4). This relay is done in pairs. The first two players in each line take this position: One puts his hands on the floor and stretches his legs out behind him. The other player stands between the legs and grips them firmly, lifting them to waist height. In this wheelbarrow position they race forward. They reverse positions at the turning line and return to their team to touch off the next pair, who have been waiting in wheelbarrow position.

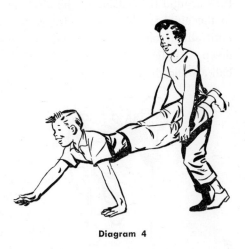

Diagram 4

**Back-to-Back Relay.** Another "pair" relay. Each first couple stands back-to-back. They hook elbows and run, either sideways or with one child moving forward and the other backward, toward the turning line. They reach this, then return to place and touch off the next couple.

**Couple-hobble Relay.** This is like the Hobble Race relay, except that it is done in pairs. The first two players in each team stand side by side. Placing his arm around his partner's waist, each lifts the knee of his outside leg, and grips the ankle of this leg with his outside hand. The couple hops toward the turning line. When they reach it, they may return to place in the same way or may simply hold hands and run back to their lines to touch off the next couple.

**Bounce-ball Relay.** Teams stand in single file behind a starting line which is about thirty feet from a wall. A "throw" line is drawn about ten feet from the wall, parallel to it. The first player in each team holds a basketball or other large ball; he runs forward to the throw line, throws the ball against the wall, and catches it on the *first* bounce. If he does not do this successfully the first time, he must repeat it until he does it correctly. He may not cross over the throw line as he does this. When he has completed the action, he runs back to place holding the ball and gives it to the next player. If the children are skilled enough, they may be asked to "dribble" the ball up to the "throw" line and back.

**Circle Relay.** Teams form single circles of equal size, facing in. The beginning player in each team has a ball or other object. At a signal he runs around the outside of the circle and back to his place, giving the ball to the child on his right. This player repeats the action. Play continues until all the children have run. The first team to complete the action sits down to indicate it has won. Older children may be asked to dribble the ball around the circle instead of simply running with it.

Diagram 5

**Dizzy-Izzy Relay** (Diagram 5). Teams stand in single file behind a starting line. The first player is given a baseball bat, broom handle, or cane at least three feet long. At a signal he runs forward. When he has crossed the turning line (about twenty-five feet away), he places his bat or cane in an upright position on the floor, touches his forehead to its upper end, and in this position runs around the bat three times. He then runs back to his team and gives the bat to the next player, who repeats the action.

**Sack Race.** In this popular stunt the first player on each team climbs into a gunny sack (any old potato, fruit, or onion burlap bag will do). Holding the open end of the sack up around his waist, he runs, jumps, or hops to the turning line and then back to touch off the next player. This may also be done as a "shuttle" race, with teams divided into two facing sections. In this a player simply crosses to the opposite group and gives the first player of that line his sack, and the two teams "shuttle" back and forth in this way.

### NOVELTY RELAYS

There are many relays which involve less strenuous physical action and require smaller play areas; these are suitable for indoor party programs.

**Cardboard Relay.** Teams stand in single file behind a starting line. Each first player is given two sheets of newspaper or, preferably, two fairly large and stiff sheets of cardboard. These may be taken from store cartons if nothing else is available. The first player must race to the turning line and back *without ever stepping directly on the floor*. He steps on one cardboard, places the other one in front of him, steps on it, places the other in front, steps on it, and so forth.

**Sir Walter Raleigh Relay** (Diagram 6). This is just the same as the Cardboard Race, except that it is done in pairs, with a girl doing the running and a boy placing the cardboards in front of her for her to travel on. The boy, of course, may touch the floor directly.

Diagram 6

**Balloon-breaking Relay.** Each first player is given a deflated toy balloon. He must blow it up, run or hop with it to the turning line, place it on the floor, sit down on it quickly to break it, and run back to his line to touch off the next player. Each player in turn repeats the action; he must not begin to blow up his balloon until the preceding player has returned to the line. This game tends to be hilarious; it is also somewhat costly in terms of burst balloons.

**Thread the Needle.** Each first player runs to a turning line or table, where there is a spool of thread and a needle. He must break off a piece of thread and thread the needle and run back to his team. Each player does this in turn. One child should be appointed as judge for each team. He stands by the table or turning line, makes sure that the needle is properly threaded, and then draws out the thread as the next player runs up. The leader should make sure that all the needles are the same size.

**Christmas-tree Relay** (Diagram 7). This game may be played in class-rooms where a large blackboard is available; otherwise a large piece of newsprint or cardboard should be tacked or taped up on the wall for each team.

Diagram 7

The first player for each team is given a piece of chalk (crayon if he is to draw on paper). He runs forward and draws the base for a Christmas tree. He returns to his line and gives the chalk to the next player, who draws the actual tree standing on the base. The third player gets the chalk and adds several Christmas tree decorations. (Decide how many in advance.) The fourth player draws several candles. (Decide number in advance.) The fifth player adds a big star at the top of the tree, and the sixth player prints "Merry Christmas" under the tree. The first team to complete the tree wins the game. Naturally the exact assignment of each player should be shown by the leader in advance.

**BALL GAMES**

Children enjoy many ball games such as baseball, basketball, football (often in modified forms such as "association" or "touch" football), soccer, and volleyball. These active sports, while they may be enjoyed in school physical education classes, are often unsuitable for informal play sessions because they usually require special play areas and equipment and teams of prescribed size. In addition, they may demand advanced playing techniques and complicated rules which children who are less than ten or eleven years of age are incapable of mastering. This chapter does not present these more formal organized team games, but instead offers a variety of what might be described as "lead-up" games. These activities give children a chance to learn certain essential skills in an uncomplicated, easygoing setting. They require little special equipment and can be played with groups of different sizes.

**Wide-awake.** All the children stand in a circle, facing the center. A volleyball or rubber playground ball is thrown from player to player in any sequence around the circle. If a child fails to catch a "fair" throw, he is eliminated. An "unfair" throw is one that is too high, too wide, or too low to be caught. The winner is the child who can remain in the game the longest.

If the leader wishes to keep all the children playing, the youngster who misses a ball may be given a point and may stay in the circle. After ten minutes the child with the lowest number of points is the winner.

**Center Catch Ball** (Diagram 8). Sometimes called "Solujee," this game is played with a single circle of children facing the center and one additional child standing inside the circle. The players standing in the circle pass a basketball or volleyball back and forth while the child in the center tries to catch it. The pass may be designated as a chest pass or a bounce pass, as the children and leader desire. If the player in the center intercepts the ball, he goes into the outer circle, while the last youngster

Diagram 8

to throw it takes his position in the center. There is no winner or loser in this game, and the leader's only concern should be to make sure that no youngster remains in the center of the circle for too long a time.

**Count the Passes.** Children divide into equal teams of six to ten players. Each team is given a basketball or volleyball and forms a single circle, facing in. At a signal the ball is passed from player to player within each circle. The object is to pass it successfully as many times as possible, counting out loud, during a given period of time. (Two or three minutes is suitable.) A dropped pass does not count. After the time has elapsed, each circle tells its score, and the winning team is given a point. The game may be played again, using a different type of pass each time.

**Balloon Push.** Two equal teams are scattered in a small gymnasium or large room. One team has one wall for a goal; the other team has the opposite wall. The teams may be marked by different colored costumes, having shirts tucked in or out, or in other ways. The leader tosses a balloon out into the center; the teams then try to work the balloon toward their own goal wall by tapping it up into the air. Each time it touches a goal wall, that team is given one point. If the balloon drops to the floor, the leader throws it up again at that point. The first team to score five or seven points is the winner.

No player is allowed to hold the ball or deliberately to shove or hold another player. In this game the balloon may be broken fairly easily; several balloons should be inflated in advance and held in reserve. A lightweight ball may also be used, but this tends to drop too easily, rather than float as a balloon does.


### INDIAN CLUB GAMES

**Indian-club Guard** (Diagram 9). A circle about twenty feet in diameter is drawn. All but one of the players stand outside the circle. Several Indian clubs are placed in a small square, rectangle, or triangle in the center of the circle, about a yard from each other. The single child in the center guards them as the other players try to knock them down with a basketball. They may pass the ball around the circle to get a good shot at the Indian clubs but may not step across the line into the circle. The player in the center tries to keep between the Indian clubs and the basketball; he may either knock the ball away directly, or if he catches it, he must throw it right back to the players outside the circle. The leader has a watch and

**Diagram 9**

times the length of time it takes the circle players to knock down all the clubs. The game is played several times, each time with a new guard in the center. The child who was able to protect the clubs for the longest time wins.

The game may also be played with two equal teams, one outside the circle trying to knock down the clubs, and the other inside guarding the clubs. The team that knocks down the clubs in the shortest time wins. Two or more balls may be used in this game, depending on the number of players and the size of the circle.

**Indian-club Bowl.** The players are divided into two equal teams, which stand in single file behind a starting line. About fifteen or twenty feet away a second parallel line is drawn. Behind this line five Indian clubs are placed, about two feet apart. Each first player is given a basketball or volleyball. He rolls this along the ground, trying to knock over an Indian club. Having bowled it, he runs up, retrieves the ball, and throws it to the next player in his line. The first player remains behind the Indian clubs as a ball boy. The others keep bowling in turn until they have knocked down all the clubs. The first team to do this is the winner.

The game may also be played with each team bowling the ball at a single club, which is replaced upright whenever it is knocked down. Each player on the team takes a turn at bowling the ball; the team that has the highest score of "knock-downs" is the winner. The first variation stresses speed; the latter emphasizes accuracy, without any time element.

**Bombardment.** A large play area is divided into two equal zones by a line drawn across the middle. Players form two equal teams; each team scatters in one of the zones. Four Indian clubs are placed at the back end of each zone, spaced about a yard apart. A basketball or other large ball is given to each team. At a signal they begin to throw the ball in an attempt to knock down their opponent's Indian clubs. Any hit counts, whether it is on the fly, after a bounce, or even on the rebound from hitting a defender. The leader should encourage the children to pass the ball from one to another, rather than try for long, direct hits.

The game may be scored by having the first team to knock down all of its opponent's Indian clubs declared the winner. Or each team may be given a point every time it knocks down a club (the club would be stood up again immediately), and the team with the most points after five minutes proclaimed the winner.

### DODGE BALL GAMES

There are many enjoyable games in which the object is to hit another player with a ball. For safety's sake the ball used should be a fairly light one, such as a volleyball or rubber playground ball, and only hits below the waist should count. There is little risk of injury when the game is played in this way. At the same time much of the child's combativeness and aggressive feeling can be worked off through this type of game.

**Team Dodge Ball.** A center line is drawn dividing a large play area in half. Two equal teams scatter, each on its own side of the center line. A ball is thrown out. One of the players retrieves it, and the game is on. The object is to eliminate as many players as possible on the opposing team by hitting them below the waist with the ball. Any child hit by the ball or stepping across the center line at any time is eliminated and must go to the side lines. The game may be scored in two ways; the team with the most players remaining after a given period of time (three to five minutes) may be the winner or the team that succeeds in completely wiping out the opposite team. If there are enough players and space, more than one ball may be used.

**Circle Dodge Ball.** Players divide into two teams. One forms a single circle with a diameter of about twenty feet, facing in. The other team scatters within the circle. The outer players are given a ball with which they attempt to hit the inner players below the waist, thus eliminating them. If the inner players are hit above the waist, it does not count. The outer-circle players may retrieve the ball by running into the circle to pick it up, but they may not throw it again until they have stepped out of the circle. The length of time it takes to eliminate all the inner players is timed by the leader. Then the teams exchange places and play again. The team which took the least amount of time to eliminate all its opponents is the winner.

**Double Dodge Ball.** This is similar to Circle Dodge Ball, in that the players divide into two equal teams. They stand, however, in a playing zone divided into three parallel areas. One team stands in the center zone; the other team divides in half and stands in the two end zones. The team that has divided attempts to eliminate the players in the center zone by hitting them below the waist with the volleyball. The game is played until the end players have eliminated all the others. Then the teams exchange zones and play the game again. The team that eliminates all its opponents in the shortest period of time wins.

Since it may be harder to wipe out all the center players in this type of formation, the game may also be played with this scoring rule: the team that wipes out the greatest number of opponents within a given time (three to five minutes) wins.

**Train Dodge Ball.** This is a variation of Circle Dodge Ball. The players form a single circle about twenty feet in diameter, facing in. Four additional players go to the center and make a Train by standing in single file, each child placing arms around the waist of the child in front of him. The player in front is the Engine, and the last player in the line is the Caboose. The players in the circle attempt to hit the Caboose below the waist with a volleyball. The Engine protects the Caboose by maneuvering the Train to keep in front of him. The Engine may also bat or kick the ball away; he is the only one in the train who may do this.

When the Caboose is finally hit by an outside player, that player takes the place of the Engine. The Engine and the other players in the Train move back one position, and the Caboose joins the players in the outer circle. The game continues in this way. There is no winner or loser, although the Engine who is able to protect his Caboose for the longest time might be considered the winner.

## OTHER BALL GAMES

**Spud.** Players stand in a small, single circle, facing in. (The circle should be about twelve feet in diameter.) One player, *It,* stands in the center of the circle, holding a volleyball or playground ball. Each player is given a number. *It* throws the ball straight up in the air, using both hands, and simultaneously calls out a number. The child whose number was called must get the ball, while all the other players, including *It,* run away. If he catches the ball on the fly, *It* must come back and begin the game again. If not, as soon as he retrieves the ball, he calls "Spud!" and all the other players must stop where they are. Then the child holding the ball throws it, trying to hit another player below the waist. The others may twist and dodge but must keep one foot fixed to the floor. If a player is hit (the ball may bounce before it hits him), he becomes *It* and the game begins again. If not, the child who threw the ball continues to be *It.* Every time a player becomes *It,* he is penalized by having a Spud against him. When a child has three Spuds he must leave the game and wait until another player has three Spuds; then he may reenter. The game may also be played without any sort of elimination or scoring, if the Spud scoring makes it too involved.

**Center Stride Ball** (Diagram 10). The players form a single circle, facing in. They take a stride position, with their feet well apart, touching the

Diagram 10

feet of their neighbors on either side. There should be enough room for a basketball or volleyball to pass easily between a player's feet.

One child stands in the center, holding a ball. He tries to throw or roll the ball so it will escape to the outside, passing between a player's feet or going between two players. The children in the circle must keep their feet fixed to the floor but use their hands to hit the ball or catch it and throw it back into the center. If the ball gets through a circle player's feet, that child is given the ball and takes the place of the center player, who takes his place in the circle. If the ball goes between two circle players (below shoulder height), the child on the right side is considered responsible and must go into the circle to begin the game.

With a large group more than one player and ball may go into the center or more than one circle may be formed.

OTHER ACTIVITIES

There are a number of other games and stunts which cannot readily be classified as tag or chase games, relays, or ball games. Some of these, such as rope jumping, hopscotch, and jacks, are usually enjoyed by smaller children, particularly girls, in very small groups in a neighborhood setting. Other activities, known as self-testing stunts, involve individual learning of physical skills and tricks but fairly large groups of children may be shown, and may experiment with, these stunts. A number of these will be presented in this section. In addition, several other games which could not be placed in any of the previous categories but are very popular with youngsters will be described here.

### GROUP GAMES AND STUNTS

**Quick Lineup.** This game may be played with as many as forty to one hundred children; it requires a large play space. The players line up in four equal lines to form a hollow square. In each line the tallest player is on the right and the others take approximate "size places" down the line. The leader stands in the middle of the square and tells the children that, no matter where he stands in the square, the number 1 line should always face him, the 2 line should be on his left, the 3 line behind him and the 4 line on his right. Each line learns its number and its correct position. The leader says, "Quick lineup!" and whirls to face in a different direction. At once all the children change places so their lines will be facing him correctly.

The first side that forms a new line, standing at attention, wins one point. The game is continued until one line scores five points and wins the game. It may be helpful to have one or two youngsters act as judges to select the winning side each time, since the leader cannot watch all the lines at once.

**Fox and Squirrel.** Form a circle of approximately fifteen or twenty children, sitting or standing. Place two objects, such as beanbags or small rubber balls, at opposite sides of the circle; one is the Squirrel and the other the Fox. At the signal, "Chase!" the children pass the Fox around the circle, trying to catch the Squirrel. Either animal may change his direction at will; so children must be alert both to help the Fox double back to catch the Squirrel by surprise and to help the Squirrel avoid his fate. There are no winners or losers in this game.

**Simon Says.** Here is one of the most popular of all childhood games. Facing the children, who stand in a block formation, the leader gives commands such as: "Jump!" "Clap hands!" "Bow!" "Bend over!" "Turn left!" "Fix your tie!" If he precedes the command with the phrase "Simon says!" the children should obey it immediately. If he does not say "Simon says!" the children should ignore the command and do nothing. If a child makes a mistake by obeying a command *without* "Simon says!" before it or ignoring one *with* "Simon says!" he is eliminated. The last child to remain in the game is the winner; if the group is very large, the remaining five or ten children may be declared the winners.

The leader should give his commands in a sharp, decisive way and so rapidly as to catch the children napping and provoke mistakes. He should also obey some commands himself and fail to obey others; this tempts them to forget to listen for "Simon says!" After children understand the game, they may take over the leader's job, which is greatly enjoyed.

**One Less.** Any number of children line up behind a starting line. About twenty feet away are piled a number of objects; these may include balls, erasers, stones, articles of clothing, etc. There should be one less article than there are children. The leader gives a signal and the youngsters run forward, each one attempting to grab an object. One child will fail to get one; he is eliminated. The game continues; each time the leader takes away one object. If a very large group is playing, the leader may take away several objects at a time and also space the objects out in a line or in several piles.

**Still Pond.** Here is a blindfold game that is suitable for a small group of young children who know each other fairly well. One youngster is blindfolded; the others scatter within a limited space with clearly marked boundaries. The blindfolded child is turned about three times. Then he calls, "Still Pond" and gropes about to find one of the other players. These youngsters may not change places, although they may bend or lean to avoid his reaching hands. When *It* locates a player, he must guess his identity by touching his face, clothes, and hair. If he guesses the name correctly, that player becomes *It*. If not, he must continue until he can find and identify another player.

### SELF-TESTING STUNTS

These activities, which stress the development of individual physical skills, are chiefly used in school physical education programs. However, they may also be presented as informal play events to small or large groups of children in playground or community-center settings. Informal dress and a casual atmosphere are needed; few self-testing activities could be used—except as possible forfeits—at a home birthday party where children are dressed-up. When a number of stunts have been learned, they might possibly be combined in a "mixed pickles" stunt relay in which each child has to perform a different, specified stunt. The chief value of the following activities lies in the pleasure children find in experimenting with interesting forms of movement and meeting new challenges; they are important, too, in improving balance, coordination, strength, and flexibility.

**Tailor Stand.** Children sit on the floor in cross-legged position. Arms are folded in front of chests, with elbows held high. At a signal each youngster tries to rise to a standing position without unfolding his arms or changing his cross-legged position. If he succeeds, he tries to sit down in the same way.

**Coffee-grinder** (Diagram 11). Each child places his right hand on the floor, keeping the arm stiff. He extends both legs out to his left and, keeping his body as straight as possible, he walks around in a circle, using his right arm as a pivot. This is repeated using the left arm as a pivot.

Diagram 11

**Bear Dance.** Children take a squatting position and extend hands straight forward for balance. The back is kept straight. Keeping weight on the left foot, each youngster thrusts his right foot forward. Then, still squatting, he brings back the right foot and thrusts the left foot forward. He does this rapidly as many times as possible. Children may informally compete to see who can do it most often, although this is not necessary. Children may also face each other in pairs and join hands; when they do it this way, they must both thrust right feet out at the same time and slightly to the side to avoid hitting each other.

**Crab Walk.** Beginning in a squatting position, each child leans back and places his hands flat on the floor. Keeping his head, neck, and trunk in as straight a line as possible (back is toward the floor) he scuttles about in a crablike way.

**Chinese Get-up** (Diagram 12). Two children sit back-to-back on the floor, arms locked with each other. They try to stand up from this position, keeping arms locked. This is a cooperative stunt in which they assist each other to rise gradually.

**Diagram 12**

**Back-to-Back Push.** Three parallel lines are marked on the floor at 10-foot intervals. Children stand in pairs on the center line. In back-to-back position they lock arms with each other. At a signal each youngster tries to push his partner across the goal line. (One pushes one way, and the other in the opposite direction.) Children should be matched as closely as possible by age and weight. The game may be scored by giving one point for each successful crossing.

**Skin the Snake.** This stunt is done in teams of equal size which compete to complete the action first. Teams stand in single file. Each child reaches down between his legs with his right arm, and grips the left hand of the child behind him. At a signal the last youngster in the line lies down on the floor. Still holding hands, the other players all back up, straddling the player on the floor. Each child, as he becomes the last in line, lies down. When every player is on his back, the last one to go down stands up and walks forward, pulling the next child up. This continues until the line is standing exactly as it was at the beginning.

Children themselves may suggest many other ways of testing such skills as throwing accuracy, speed, dodging, jumping, etc. These activities are most useful after the age of eight or nine and tend to be somewhat more popular with boys than girls. Here are several examples.

**Five Jumps.** Children stand with their toes on a starting line. At a signal each child jumps five times forward. Each child may measure the distance he has covered with a piece of chalk and try again to improve his score. Or it may be played as a game, with the child farthest from the starting line being declared the winner.

**Ball in the Basket.** Children line up in equal teams on a throwing line. About ten feet away from each team is a wastepaper basket. The first player in each team has a beanbag or 8-inch play ball. Each child takes his turn at trying to throw the ball in the basket. When a team has finished, it adds up its score; the top team wins. The scoring may be more satisfactory if the basket is placed within a small circle marked on the floor. If the ball lands within the basket, the score may be five points; if it hits the basket without dropping in, it may be worth three points; if it lands within the circle, it may be given one point.

**Cross the Creek.** Two parallel lines drawn about two feet apart are the "creek." Children line up in single file and follow the leader in jumping or leaping across it. After each youngster has crossed the "creek," it is widened by about six inches. Again they follow the leader. When children fail to make it across, they are out of the game. The "creek" is continually widened until only the winner remains.

**Beneath the Bar.** A very similar game is one in which a crossbar is held beneath two supports. In pairs, children walk beneath this. The bar is gradually lowered (two or three inches at a time) until it is so low that the children must crawl under. The rule is that they must maintain contact with their partners and may not touch the crossbar as they go under. Couples are gradually eliminated; the last pair to inch its way under is the winner.

# CHAPTER 6

# PARTY GAMES
# AND MIXERS

This chapter offers a variety of games, stunts, and social mixers that may be enjoyed by children at indoor parties, where space is somewhat limited. In general they may be used throughout the entire six-through-twelve age range, although younger children would not do too well in the quiz and other mental games, and twelve-year-olds would not enjoy such simple games as "I See Blue." It is up to the leader to use his best judgment as to which games are suitable for his group. When necessary, he should feel free to adapt or modify a game so that it will be more interesting for the children he is working with.

The activities in this chapter fall into these categories: social games and mixers; mental quizzes, puzzles and magic stunts; drawing games; and equipment games. They appear in approximate order of difficulty.

### SOCIAL GAMES AND MIXERS

When a party is getting under way and children enter one or two at a time, it is a good idea to present some sort of "ice-breaker" in which they can become involved immediately. These "ice-breakers" should require little instruction or organization.

**Yes or No.** Each child, as he enters, is given ten or fifteen beans or grains of dried corn. Youngsters are instructed to ask each other all sorts of questions. Any child who makes a reply with a "yes" or "no" in it must pay the questioner one bean or grain. The game continues for about ten minutes. The child who has amassed the greatest number of beans or grains is the winner.

**Odd or Even.** As in the previous game, each child is given ten or fifteen beans or grains of corn to begin with. Any youngster goes up to another, holding his clenched hand in front of him and saying, "Odd or even?" The other child makes a choice, and the first youngster opens his hand to show whether he has been holding an odd or an even number of beans. If the second child has made a correct guess, the first one must give him the beans he had in his hand. If the guess was incorrect, the second child has to give the first the number of beans the first child had. The game continues for several minutes; the winner is the one who has harvested the biggest crop.

**Meet My Friend.** In a group of children who do not know each other very well, each youngster is asked to find out the name of a person new to him—and also to learn such details as where he lives, where he goes to school, what his hobbies are, how old he is, etc. Then, after some time has gone by, introductions are in order. Each child in turn rises and introduces his new friend to the entire group, telling in a loud voice everything he has learned about him. To ensure every child's being introduced, it might be wise to have the children sit in a circle and have each youngster find out about and introduce the neighbor on his right.

**I See Blue.** One child secretly selects an object in the room or immediate vicinity which all the children can see. He says, "I see blue" (or whatever the color of the object actually is). One at a time the other children try to guess what the object is. It may be a piece of furniture, part of a picture hanging on the wall, or an article of clothing. The first child to guess it becomes the leader and selects a new object.

**Dog and Bone** (Diagram 13). The players sit in a fairly large circle, facing in. One child sits on the floor in the center, with his eyes closed and

Diagram 13

with any small object right beside him. He is the Dog, and the object is the Bone. Any child in the sitting circle points at another, who then tries to creep up and steal the Bone, without the Dog's hearing him. If the Dog hears the creeping child at any time, he points at the direction of the sound. If he points reasonably accurately at the would-be Thief, that child must put the Bone back and return to place. If the Thief is able to get the Bone back to his place without being detected, he has won, and becomes the new Dog as the game is played over. Ideally, this game should be played on a wood floor which tends to creak slightly, because a grass or concrete surface makes it too easy for the Thief to creep up unheard. Also, all the children must remain quite quiet to give the Dog a fair chance to hear each Thief.

**Observation.** A number of varied objects (fifteen or twenty) are placed on a table. The children march past, one at a time. Then the objects are covered with a sheet or put away, and the children are asked to write down the names of as many of the articles as they can remember. The child who remembers the greatest number is the winner.

**Automobile.** The children sit in a circle. The leader stands in the center and gives each child the name of some part of an automobile—wheel, tire, windshield wiper, mirror, engine, window, lights, clutch, brake, seat, etc. If there are a large number of participants, there may be two or three of each part. The leader then tells an exciting story of an automobile ride. When he names any part of a car, the player or players referred to must stand up, clap hands, turn around, and sit down. He names as many parts as he can in rapid succession. Then he suddenly exclaims, "And the automobile went over a cliff and was *wrecked*!" At the word "wrecked," each child must jump up and take a new seat. The leader is quick to take a chair, so one child is left standing. He becomes the new leader as the game is played again.

**Shoe Scramble.** Each child takes his shoes off, places them in a mixed-up pile in the center of the room, and then stands facing a wall. At a signal all the youngsters race to the pile and try to find their own shoes and put them on. When a child has completely laced his shoes, he runs back to the wall. The first child to complete the action is the winner. This game tends to result in roughhousing (such as throwing shoes out the window or hiding them in very hard-to-find places) and should be kept under control. Also it should not be played too often.

**Life-saver Horse Race** (Diagram 14). Several children volunteer to take part in a "horse race." Each youngster is given a piece of string about two feet long at the end of which has been tied a life-saver or other small piece of candy. The children place the free end of the string between their teeth so the candy dangles at the other end. At a signal they put their hands behind their backs and try to draw the string up into their mouths. The first child to get the candy in his mouth is the winner. They quickly learn the technique of getting it up with an action similar to chewing, but they should be warned against swallowing it. The strings should be exactly the same length and should, of course, be kept quite clean before using.

Diagram 14

**Fanning Football** (Diagram 15). A goal line is drawn or indicated at each end of the room, and children are divided into two teams. These teams then scatter over the entire floor, taking spots which they must not leave. Each child is given a paper fan, and a ping-pong ball is thrown into the center. By vigorous fanning or blowing each team tries to send the ball across the opponent's goal line. Each touchdown counts six points. If a player accidentally touches the ball, his team loses one point.

The game may also be played with children being given rolled-up newspapers. Players are allowed actually to hit the ping-pong ball, as in hockey, but must still stay fixed to an assigned spot.

Diagram 15

**Scavenger Hunt.** One of the most popular and traditional party stunts is to divide a group into several teams and give each team a list of objects to gather. If it is an indoor party, the objects should be the sort players might have in pockets or easily available, such as combs, pencils, tops, balls, hairpins, shoelaces, etc. If players are permitted to roam, the list of items may be much more varied, difficult, and humorous. The older the children are, the tougher the list may be made and the longer the period of time given to carry out the Scavenger Hunt.

**Baby-picture Contest.** Each youngster is asked in advance to bring a picture of himself as a baby. The pictures are numbered and tacked to the wall without other identification. Children go around with paper and pencil and try to guess the correct name to go with each picture. When everyone has had a fair chance to guess at each photo, the identities are given. The winner is the child with the most correct names.

**How Many?** Before the children come, the leader fills a large bottle, bowl, or other transparent container with beans, grains of corn, or pebbles. He alone knows how many there are. Each child writes down his guess as to the number of objects in the container (after examining it from every side). He submits the guess on a slip with his name on it. When all the slips are in, the leader tells the correct number. The child who made the closest guess is the winner.

**Secret Names.** Each child, as he enters, has the name of a famous person pinned on his back by the leader. He is also given a piece of paper and a pencil. He must try to find out who the other famous people in the room are by getting close enough to them to read the slips on their backs. And since it is a contest to see who can list the most correct names, he tries to prevent others from seeing the slip on his back, by backing against a wall or even, in some cases, quickly lying down. This game results in much running, chasing, ducking, and dodging as children try to sneak up behind each other to read the slips. After about ten minutes, time is called, and the child with the longest list is declared the winner.

**Poison Penny.** Children sit or stand around in a circle, facing in, while music is played on a piano or phonograph. A penny is passed around the circle from child to child as quickly as possible. When the music stops suddenly, whoever is holding the penny is eliminated. If no music is available, the leader may beat a drum or blow a whistle to indicate the fatal moment. Objects other than pennies may, of course, be used, and if the group is very large, several objects at once may be passed, so that several players may be eliminated at once.

**Hidden Coin.** This is similar to the previous game. Children sit or stand in a circle. In rhythm they extend their hands to their neighbors, joining hands for a moment with them, and then bring their own hands together. As they do this, they pass a coin, preferably a fairly large one such as a half dollar or silver dollar, from person to person. One child stands in the center and tries to guess who is holding the concealed coin at any given moment. If he guesses correctly, he changes places with this child. If not, he is given two more chances; then a new *It* is chosen. If children are standing, they may play the game by passing the coin around behind their backs.

**Shouted Proverbs.** Children divide into two or more teams. Each team, meeting by itself, selects a proverb. Each child in the team is given one word of the proverb. The teams then face each other. Members of one team all shout their individual words; those on the other team try to make out as many words as possible and then guess the proverb. When they have succeeded in doing this, they take their turn and shout out their proverb.

**Trading Proverbs.** In advance the leader writes a number of proverbs on slips of paper and cuts each slip into three or four pieces. These slips are then distributed in quantity around the room, under chairs, on tables, on the floor, and even pinned to the wall. At a signal each child gathers as many slips as he can. Then, by putting together the slips (he may also trade with other children), he tries to assemble as many complete proverbs as possible. After ten or fifteen minutes the game is ended, and the child with the greatest number of completed sayings reads them aloud.

In preparing the slips the leader may be wise to use only five or six different proverbs, making several copies of each. Also, when cutting them up, he should be careful not to cut through words, which would make it doubly difficult to assemble slips.

**Who Am I?** One player leaves the room while the others name him for some familiar or famous person, living or dead; he is the only person who does not now know his identity. He comes back in and tries to find out who he is by asking such questions as, "Am I alive?" "Am I a man?" "Am I famous as a sports figure?" Questions must call for "yes" or "no" replies, rather than additional information. Gradually he narrows down the field. He is allowed three guesses as to his identity. If he succeeds in guessing it, the last child to give him a reply is the new *It*. If not, he may become *It* again or the group may select a new *It*.

**Hold Fast** (Diagram 16). One player is the leader; the other children divide into groups of four. Each group stands in a small square, holding a handkerchief (one player holds each corner). When the leader calls out, "Let go!" the players must hold fast to the handkerchief. When he calls

"Hold fast!" they must all let go. He begins by giving the orders fairly slowly, and gradually speeds up. After a practice period, the game is played in earnest. Any child who makes a mistake drops out, until there is only

Diagram 16

one youngster left who is still holding a handkerchief. He is the winner and becomes the new leader.

**Lists of Forfeits.** Many games may be played with children being asked to pay a forfeit. This should be humorous but not embarrassing or dangerous; if the leader feels that it is in any way harmful to the children, it should be discontinued. Here are several forfeits which children enjoy and which are generally acceptable.

1. Do an imitation of a popular television or movie star.

2. Pat your stomach with one hand while rubbing your head with the other.

3. Face somebody else; yawn until you can make them yawn, or laugh until you can make them laugh.

4. Make a one-minute speech on an assigned topic.

5. Say rapidly five times a tongue twister such as "Peter Piper picked a peck of pickled peppers."

6. Show how you can snore five different ways.

7. Tell the others, in a thirty-second speech, how wonderful you think you are.

8. Show your acting versatility by laughing, crying, frowning, and smiling, all within thirty seconds.

9. Give sincere compliments to five other players.

**Musical Chairs.** This is perhaps the most familiar of all party games and is enjoyed by all ages. All the children take chairs and place them in a line, down the length of the room. The chairs face in alternate directions. At a signal the children walk counterclockwise around the chairs to the accompaniment of a piano or phonograph. One chair is withdrawn from the line by the leader. The music stops—and every child rushes to get a seat. The child who is unable to get a chair is the loser. The game is repeated until only the winner remains. If a very large group is playing, several chairs may be withdrawn at a time, so several children will be eliminated at once.

**Airplane.** The leader tacks on the wall a large map of the world or a drawing of it. Each child is given a small airplane cut out of paper, with his name printed on it and a pin in it. One central country of the map is marked as the Landing Field. Children stand at the opposite end of the room; each child is given a chance to look at the location of the Landing Field and at several articles of furniture (obstacles) which are scattered through the room. One at a time youngsters are blindfolded; they must then cross the room and pin their airplanes as close as possible to the Landing Field. If they accidentally touch any obstacle, it is considered a Crash and they are out of the race. If the airplane lands in water on the map, it is also a Crash and they are eliminated. The child who is closest to the Landing Field wins.

**Blackboard Baseball** (Diagram 17). A diagram is drawn on the blackboard if the game is to be played in a classroom, or on a large sheet of cardboard or plywood if it is to be played elsewhere. There are nine or more boxes marked home run, strike out, base on balls, etc.

| BASE ON BALLS | DOUBLE PLAY | SINGLE |
|---|---|---|
| GROUNDER (OUT AT FIRST) | HOME RUN | STRIKE OUT |
| DOUBLE | FLYBALL CAUGHT | TRIPLE |

Diagram 17

Children divide into two teams and one team comes to bat. The first child throws an eraser at the blackboard. (The chalk dust makes a mark.) If a cardboard or plywood sheet is being used, children may use suction darts; or a soft lump of clay, which will stick when it hits the board. From this point on the game is played like baseball. A box score is kept. Each team is allowed three outs per inning, and the game may be played for seven or nine innings. The game may be dramatized by actually setting up a home plate and three bases in the room (chairs will do as markers) and having children walk through the motions after making their throws, but this is not essential.

NOTE: The double-play box only counts if there is a runner at first. Otherwise it is considered a routine "out" play at first.

## MENTAL GAMES, QUIZZES, AND PUZZLES

At parties for older children, inactive games of a quiz or guessing variety are likely to be very popular, particularly because so many of these have been featured recently over television. It is always more fun to do rather than just to watch, and children know this! No party should consist entirely of mental games, but they will fit in well after a session of active games or dancing. In each game the quiz questions or other subject matter should depend, of course, on the maturity and grade level of the children who are to play it. The wise leader will recognize that the examples offered in this book are merely illustrations and will make up questions that are within the range of knowledge and interest of his own children.

**Brain Teasers.** Children are given pieces of paper and pencils, and the following problems are tried:

1. Each child is asked to write down and number as many of the forty-eight states as possible. The winner is the child who has the greatest number after five minutes. Other subjects: state capitals, countries of the world, bodies of water, fish, flowers, animals, Presidents of the United States, etc.

2. A short selection is played from each of ten or fifteen popular phonograph records. Children must write down the title; the youngster with the greatest number of correct identifications wins.

3. Famous dates are named. EXAMPLES: 1898 (Spanish American War); 1776 (Declaration of Independence); 1941 (World War II); 1066 (Battle of Hastings). The child who correctly identifies the greatest number on his paper wins.

4. A list of famous nicknames is read off slowly, one at a time. EXAMPLES: Buffalo Bill (Colonel William Cody); The Bronx Bombers (New York Yankees); The Lone Eagle (Charles Lindbergh); The Brown Bomber (Joe Louis); The Brockton Blockbuster (Rocky Marciano); Ike (Dwight Eisenhower); Old Hickory (Andrew Jackson). The child who correctly identifies the most names on his sheet is the winner.

NOTE: The leader will find an encyclopedia invaluable in preparing his own questions. Also, some of the children themselves may help prepare quiz questions; of course, these children would not take part in the game.

**Team Quizzes.** Another useful type of mental game is the team quiz, in which youngsters divide into opposing teams of equal size. If the over-all group is quite small, each youngster may be on a team. If it is large, only eight or ten children may play the game and the others temporarily act as an audience. Teams may be set up on the basis of boys vs. girls, children from different schools opposing each other, or children from different neighborhoods opposing each other. In beginning the game, teams should sit as units, one team on each side of the leader, who acts as master of ceremonies. If the contestants do not know each other too well, it may be wise to have them have placards with their names printed in large letters on their laps or on a table in front of them. The leader may introduce the children to each other and explain the rules.

The actual asking and answering of questions may be done in these ways:

1. When the leader asks a question, each child may ring a bell or raise his hand when he thinks he has the correct answer. The first child to signal is permitted to answer. If he is correct, his team gets a point. If not, the opposing team gets a point. The important thing here is to avoid a wild hubbub in which children shriek the answer in unison, for this makes it difficult to score the answer and children will often angrily accuse the leader of unfairness. They must *not* reply until the leader indicates which child has signaled first and may offer an answer.

2. Another way is to have players on alternate teams take turns at replying to the questions. For instance, the first question may go to the first player on Team A, the next to the first player on Team B, the next to the second player on Team A, and so on. A variation of this is to permit a player on one team to attempt to answer it if a player on the other team was unable to.

3. A third way is to permit a team to huddle each time and come up with a collective reply, but this is not often done.

The subject matter for team quizzes is very broad, of course. Here are some typical examples which should appeal to children.

**Sports Quizzes.** Children may be asked questions about championship teams, about players who hold certain records, and about the rules of different sports and games. They may be asked to identify players by their nicknames.

**Animal Quizzes.** Children may be asked to give the names of animals beginning first with "A," then "B," then "C," etc.

The leader may give the word for the male of a species, and ask children to name the female corresponding to it. EXAMPLES: Drake — duck; boar — sow; stallion — mare; gander — goose; rooster — hen, etc.

The leader may name an animal and ask children to identify the sound it makes. EXAMPLES: frogs — croak; geese — honk; owls — hoot; cats — meow; coyotes — howl; donkeys — bray; sheep — bleat.

The leader may ask children to identify the young of different species. EXAMPLES: lion — cub; goose — gosling; deer — fawn; seal — calf; frog — pollywog; sheep — lamb; horse — colt; bear — cub.

**Geography Quiz.** The leader may ask children to give the capital cities of different states as he names them.

He may ask them to identify the countries that certain rivers flow in.

He may ask them to identify certain states according to facts about them. EXAMPLES: largest state (Texas); smallest state (Rhode Island); state with largest population (New York); state with longest coastline (California); etc.

He may ask them to give the location of certain mountain ranges, famous deserts, and natural wonders.

**Famous Sayings.** The leader may quote a famous statement and give several possible sources, of which the children must pick the right one.

EXAMPLES: "Go west, young man."
    Daniel Boone  Horace Greeley  Davy Crockett
    "I only regret that I have but one life to give to my country."
    Benedict Arnold  The Unknown Soldier  Nathan Hale

**Music Quiz.** The leader may name or play part of famous songs and ask children to identify the opera, movie, or musical show the song came from. He may hum a tune, give part of a line, and ask children to complete the line. Using folk songs, which are better for this purpose since they continue to be well known by children year after year, he might ask such questions as:

Who was bitten by the Bluetail Fly? ANSWER: my master.
What covered Old Smoky?    ANSWER: snow.
Who fought the Battle of Jericho? ANSWER: Joshua.

NOTE: These quiz questions are merely suggestions. The leader who wishes to use quizzes with children can either make up his own lists of questions from encyclopedias, sports reference books, maps, and the like, or he may draw them from already existing book collections of quizzes.

The danger here is that quizzes may be dated and many of the answers not known by today's youngsters. Therefore all quiz material should be subject to a rigid scrutiny to see if most of the questions will be fairly familiar to most of the participants.

## OTHER MENTAL GAMES

There are many other mental games and stunts which children may play. Here are several additional ones.

**Spelling Contest.** Children divide into two or more equal teams. The teams stand in single file on a starting line. About ten feet away on chairs or a table are piles of shuffled cards. (Each card has a large letter of the alphabet printed on it.) There is one pile for each team. The leader calls out a word of about four or five letters; it should be fairly simple to spell. The first child in each line runs up and searches in his pile of cards for the first letter of the word. He finds it and runs back to his line. Facing them, he holds the card across his chest. The next child runs up to find the next letter. The first team to spell the word correctly and completely wins one point. The cards are replaced in the piles, and the children who have just been active go to the foot of their line. The leader calls out a new word and new children run up to find the letters. The first team to get a fixed number of points (five is about right) wins.

**Word-making Race.** Each child is given a card with a letter on it. All the players are divided into two or more equal teams. (Each team has the same letters.) The children are asked to make up as many words using these letters as they can within five minutes, listing them on a sheet of paper as they make them up. The words must be at least three letters long. After the allotted time, the team with the highest number of words reads its list.

**One Minute, Please.** Children divide into two equal teams in facing rows. The leader assigns one child a subject to talk on—and he must talk for one minute on that subject without repeating himself or bringing in other topics. (Naturally, he will not always make sense.) Then the leader asks a child from the other team to talk on another assigned subject under the same conditions. When they have both chattered for one minute, the onlookers vote by applause to show which one they felt did the best job. The game is continued, with a new topic being given to each participant. The leader should make up in advance a good list of nonsensical topics, such as "Eating habits of the polar bear," "Why girls would make good weight-lifters," "How to thread a needle with a thick rope," etc.

**Mixed-up Names.** Children are divided into two equal teams. The leader holds up a placard with a "scrambled" or mixed-up word on it. The first child to unscramble it and give the correct name or word is the winner and gets a point for his team. EXAMPLES: hocslo (school); ciums (music); labtolof (football). Names tend to be somewhat more difficult. Christopher Columbus, for instance, becomes Sterichorph Busculom. Words must be carefully selected and scrambled so they are neither so simple that several children get them immediately nor so difficult that no one can get them.

### DRAWING GAMES

There are a number of novelty games in which drawing is the basis of the activity. Artistic ability is definitely *not* needed to play these games— and the leader should make this clear at once.

**What Is It?** This game may be played in a classroom where there is a blackboard; otherwise sheets of newsprint may be tacked or taped up along the walls. The leader writes on slips of paper the names of as many animals as there are children playing the game. Each child takes one of the slips. Each child in turn goes to the board and draws with chalk or crayon the animal he has been assigned. The other children guess what he has drawn and write it down on their own sheets of paper. Finally all the drawings are named by the leader, and the player with the most correct identifications is the winner.

**Blind Pig.** All children are blindfolded and given paper and pencil. They are asked to draw a pig without lifting the pencil from the paper except, when they are finished, to draw the eye where they think it belongs. They take their blindfolds off and vote for the drawing they think is best.

**Crazy Drawing.** Each child is given a sheet of paper and a pencil. He draws a single line on his paper; the line may be straight, curved, or crooked. At a signal each paper is passed to the right. The children add a second line to the first one. This is continued, the object being to develop, if possible, recognizable drawings. After eight or ten passes to the right, the drawings are held up and exhibited. Some of the pictures will have obvious form and meaning; others are likely to be quite abstract. The leader may find that the children prefer working with colored crayons and that the finished crayon drawings are likely to be bolder and more effective.

**Progressive Artists.** Each child is given paper and pencil and begins the game by drawing a head (of a man, woman, or child) at the top of the sheet. Then, at the leader's signal, he folds over the paper so that the head is hidden but part of the neck shows. Papers are all passed to the right. Each child is asked to draw the next part of the body including the chest, shoulders, and arms (down to the belt). Again the sheet is folded over so only the belt shows. It is passed to the right and the next player draws from the belt to the knees. It is folded once more and the next player finishes the drawing. Papers are passed back to the original artist, who displays the "work of art" he had begun.

### MAGIC STUNTS

So-called "magic stunts" have entertainment value at parties; they may be carried on in two ways. One requires a fairly skilled performer who puts on a real show, with card tricks, rabbits, scarves, and professional equipment. Not only does this kind of entertainment depend on the group's ability to get such a performer to volunteer his services, but it results in a passive kind of experience for most of the children, who sit and watch without being involved. The second kind of magic entertainment consists of simple tricks or stunts which may be easily demonstrated by the leader and which children may try for themselves or of "mind-reading" magic which the leader rehearses in advance with a secret accomplice and which actually requires no special skill at all. This second type of magic entertainment is much easier to present and, while it may not be as spectacular as the first kind, brings about broader participation in the group.

Here are several sample stunts which the leader may try at a children's party.

**Black Magic.** The leader must have an accomplice in this "mind-reading" stunt. He tells the children that he can ask someone to leave the room and then, when he has returned, give him a message through sheer "brain waves" about an object the other children chose while he was out. The accomplice (who has been trained by the leader in advance) goes out, and the children pick an object. The leader then names several objects, one at a time, using the phrase, "Is it this?" When he names the correct

object, the accomplice says, "Yes, that's the one." The secret is that the
leader preceded mention of the correct object by naming a black article.
The game may be played using different colors as the "give-away" clue, and
further to confuse the participants, the leader may have worked out an
American-flag sequence (red, then white, then blue) with his accomplice.

In this, as in all such stunts, the leader may encourage the children
to guess how it is done, to try to do it themselves, and, at the end, may tell
them the secret if he wishes to do so.

**The Hypnotized Knee.** The leader announces that he can hypnotize
the knee of anyone in the room so that he actually cannot lift it. When a
child volunteers, he has him stand with his *right* side against the wall; as
much of the body as possible (foot, leg, hip, arm, and shoulder) must
actually be touching the wall. Then the leader makes some magic passes,
utters a few gobbledegook incantations, and says, "You cannot lift your
*left* leg because the knee is hypnotized. Try it." The child actually will be
unable to lift the left leg, not because of hypnosis, of course, but because
the position makes it impossible. This is a highly amusing and effective
stunt; the leader may do it with several children in a row.

**Secret Cities.** This stunt is similar to Black Magic, except that when
the accomplice goes out, the group picks the name of a city, which the
leader must try to convey by "brain waves" on his return. When the accomplice comes in, the leader says a list of name of cities slowly. When he
says the correct one, the accomplice smiles and says, "That's it! I feel
the brain waves." Actually, the secret is that the leader precedes the name
of the chosen city with the name of a two-part city, such as San Francisco
or New Orleans. To make it harder to detect the name may come *two*
places after a two-part cities or after *two* two-part cities have been mentioned.

**What's the Color?** The leader says that he can tell the color of a
crayon behind his back. He gives six crayons to any child in the group and
asks him to hide five of them and wrap the other one up in a paper napkin
and hand it to him. The child does this. The leader takes the completely
hidden crayon, holds it behind his back for a moment, and then takes it
out (still covered by the paper). He identifies the color correctly and then
reveals the crayon to show he is right. How? While the crayon is behind
his back, the leader quickly takes it out of the napkin and scrapes a little
off on his thumbnail. Then he replaces it in the paper and brings it out.
His back is to the group so they cannot see this. He can easily see the speck

of crayon on his thumbnail—and thus can tell the color of the crayon. Markedly different colors should be used, such as white, black, blue, green, yellow, and red; dark colors tend to look too much alike.

**Magic Cane.** The leader shows a cane to the group and says that with its magic assistance he will convey a message to one of the children. His accomplice goes out of the room, and the leader asks the other children to pick a short verb, such as "sing," "dance," "run," or "hop." They do this. The accomplice returns and the leader goes through a routine of waving the cane in the air, tapping on the floor, and making short statements. Apparently the verb is communicated, because the accomplice acts it out.

The secret is that the leader spells the word out for the accomplice in two ways. The vowels are communicated by cane taps on the flour: A (one tap), E (two taps), I (three taps), O (four taps) and U (five taps). Consonants are shown through the first letter in each of the leader's statements.

For the word "hop," the leader might begin: "Have a seat, Bob." Then he taps four times, for "O." Then, "Please, everybody, I must have complete quiet." H-O-P is spelled out and the accomplice begins to hop about.

This stunt, like most magic tricks of its kind, would probably be more interesting for slightly older children, who could play it for themselves when the leader had explained it.

### EQUIPMENT GAMES

There is a wealth of equipment or "board" games such as checkers, Parcheesi, Monopoly, Anagrams, and others, which serve for quiet indoor play of small groups of children. Usually such games contain their own direction sheets when purchased or are taught by one child to another without need for adult leadership. Therefore there would be little point to including them in this book.

In addition, however, there are many other kinds of equipment games which children enjoy and for which they can often construct or improvise the needed materials. These homemade games may simply be left in a playroom for occasional use or may be set up as side-line activities at special parties or carnivals. Here are several examples of games which can be homemade.

**Hammer Board.** A number of nails are partly driven into a thick board placed across some sawhorses so that they are securely fixed but at least two or three inches of each nail still protrudes. Each child takes his turn at driving the nail into the plank with an ordinary hammer. This may be played in two ways: seeing how many blows it takes to drive the nail completely in, or seeing which child drives the nail in the farthest with a single blow.

**Shoot Out the Candle.** A wax candle is lighted and placed on a plate or tray on a table, about six or eight feet behind a restraining rope or board. Each child is given a full water pistol with which to shoot out the candle flame. If he succeeds, he wins a certain number of points. The game may also be played with several candles at a greater distance.

**In the Hat.** An ordinary felt hat is placed upside down on the ground. Children stand behind a line about a yard away. Each child is given ten playing cards; one at a time he tries to flip these into the hat. If this is too difficult, he may be permitted to stand directly over the hat to toss the cards.

**In the Bottle.** This is a very similar game, in which a child kneels on an ordinary kitchen chair, resting his right forearm on the back of the chair. A milk bottle is placed on the floor behind the chair, and the child is given five clothespins to drop into the bottle.

**Match This.** Each child is given a soda straw and five safety matches. He stands about four feet from a frying pan which has been placed on a low table or chair. Using the straw as a beanshooter, he tries to blow the matches into the pan one at a time.

**Bottle Ten Pins.** Ten soda or catsup bottles are set up in a triangle (just like pins in a bowling alley). Each child stands about fifteen feet away and rolls a fairly large rubber ball to bowl over the pins. If he knocks them all over the first time, he is given a bonus score; if not, he is given a second chance and then given a certain score for each pin knocked over.

**Can Ball.** Five large coffee cans are fastened to a large sheet of plywood and every can is given a score value. The board is leaned against the wall or placed on a chair or easel. Each child stands ten feet away and is given five small beanbags, balls, or other objects of a suitable size. He throws the objects at the board one at a time and adds up successful throws for a total score.

**Ring the Bell.** A small bell is suspended in a 12- or 15-inch diameter wire hoop which is hung from an open doorway or ceiling so it is at eye-level height. The hoop should be so fixed that it does not turn and provides a stationary target. Children stand about ten feet away and take turns throwing a rubber ball at the hoop. If the ball goes through the hoop without hitting the bell, the child may be given ten points. If it hits the bell, the score may be reduced to five points. *Or,* hitting the bell may be given a bonus score. Each child is allowed several throws.

**Bounce the Ball.** Children stand about twelve or fifteen feet from a wastepaper basket or box which has been placed on the floor. Each child is given several tries to bounce a rubber or tennis ball into the basket; it must bounce once after he throws it and then drop in. The game may also be played so that he bounces the ball on the floor so it will hit a wall and drop into a basket which has been placed before the wall.

**Funnel Ball.** Each child is given a small rubber ball and a funnel. Facing a wall (about ten feet from it) he must throw the ball with his right hand so it hits the floor and then the wall. Holding the funnel in his left hand, he must catch the ball in it on its rebound from the wall. Each child is given several tries and may move from his position to catch the ball in the funnel.

## Progressive Game Contest

The preceding equipment games may be played by large groups of children in this way; they are divided up into smaller teams of equal size, which rotate in playing games and contests which are spaced around a large room or gymnasium. Each child is given a score card with his name on it, a place for the name of each game he will play, and a space for his score in each game. Teams go from game to game (suitable scores have been worked out for each game) and an official scorer and leader help them take part in each game. They need not play the games in any special order. After perhaps an hour or so, when each team has taken part in all the games, the children with the highest total scores are declared the winners, either on a team or individual basis.

## Winning and Losing

The goal of winning should not be made the most important aspect of team play; the fun of the game and of doing one's best should be of primary concern and losing should never be made a disgrace. Nonetheless, the wise leader will recognize that children enjoy a certain amount of clean-cut competition and that it heightens the interest they take in any game. The spice of victory, even when it is just over one's preceding score, cannot be denied.

Thus, in most of the preceding games there is a certain element of competition and, at the end, a statement that one child is the winner. With this in mind, the leader should endeavor to provide such a wide variety of games and activities that almost every child can find some activity that he can excel in. Secondly, no prizes should ever be given that are valuable because of their intrinsic worth. When prizes are awarded, they should be nothing more than a little hand-painted scroll, an inexpensive token which may be purchased in the 5-and-10-cent store, or a joke prize based on the game—such as a shiny red apple given to the winner of the apple-dunking contest.

At all times, in playing these games, the leader should be aware of the reactions of the children and the nature of the social experience they seem to be having and should be responsive to their ideas and suggestions as to how activities may be carried on.

# CHAPTER 7

# FOLK DANCES

# AND

# SINGING GAMES

Young children take great pleasure in vigorous, rhythmic activity. For this reason, and also because it is such a lively, social kind of experience, dance is one of the most popular forms of childhood play. Children may enjoy two chief kinds of dance while they are in the elementary grades: traditional and creative.

*Traditional.* This includes singing games and play parties, and folk, square, and ballroom dances, all of which have set formations, step movements, and sequences, and which are taught *to* children. Since traditional dancing is usually an easily controlled and directed form of play, even leaders with little experience can work effectively with it with small or large groups of children.

*Creative.* Various forms of dance, rhythmic, and dramatic play in which children are encouraged to express themselves freely through movement are included under this heading. The stress is usually on discovering and expanding the range of the child's bodily movement and on stimulating self-expression and emotional release. The resulting dance form may be completely abstract and free of literal meaning or may attempt to communicate specific ideas through movement.

Of course no single form of dance is, or should be, completely traditional *or* creative, and no teacher should try to make it so.

In many folk dances and singing games children are encouraged to develop their own style of movement and even, in some dances, to improvise steps on the spur of the moment. On the other hand, creative dance

89

activities often borrow rhythms and movement skills directly from folk and other traditional sources.

It is possible to present both types of dance activity to children in a single play session or continuing experience; often they may be blended in a single expression. However, they are more easily described when dealt with separately, so that procedure is followed in this book. A variety of traditional dances are described in this chapter. The following chapter covers creative dance techniques.

## Traditional Dance Forms

The simplest kind of prestructured dance activity is the singing game or nursery rhyme to which pantomimic action has been fitted. These are most useful with children in kindergarten or the primary grades.

The play party is a form of singing game which was developed in American pioneer days (often using tunes brought from abroad) and which was originally used by teen-agers and young adults for social fun. Since play parties are usually uncomplicated and are highly rhythmical and jolly in spirit, they are suitable for use with children from about the second or third grade and up.

Simple folk dances of European nations are also popular. They are done in many formations and combinations and usually involve simple actions clearly fitted to folk music. A few such dances may be done in primary grades, but the majority are suited for intermediate and even later levels.

During the intermediate grades children may begin to enjoy square dancing, particularly if they have done many play parties, since the action is quite similar. Also, in the fifth and sixth grades children may find success in learning basic folk dance steps like the polka and schottische. At this same time, in many schools and communities, children also begin to learn ballroom dance steps like the fox trot or waltz.

## How to Select Suitable Dances

Inevitably, the classroom teacher, play leader, or parent who is unskilled in dance will ask, "How do I pick dances that will be right for the children I work with? They shouldn't be so hard they can't do them—or so simple they won't enjoy them!"

In the past collections of dances often assigned dances to specific ages, which was one way of answering this problem. Today, because we realize that children vary greatly in their abilities and interests, we feel that it is safer to assign a dance to an age span such as fourth and fifth grades. It is also helpful for a play leader to be able to judge for himself whether a dance will be suitable for a particular group of children. He should check the following points:

*Difficulty of Steps.* Primary grade children can usually do walking, skipping, running, stamping, jumping, or clapping; but if steps like the polka, waltz, mazurka, or schottische are included, dances should not be presented before the fifth or sixth grade, or even later.

*Length of Dance.* Younger children should not do dances with more than one or two different actions, although older children may learn and remember several different sequences in a dance.

*Music.* The speed and rhythmic complexity of a dance's accompanying music may make it unsuitable for young children.

*Formation.* Complex formations or difficult partner-changing may make a dance suitable only for older children.

*Make-believe.* If a dance has storytelling movements such as winding flax or scolding a partner, it may be better for little children than older ones, who may be embarrassed by what they consider childish actions.

The leader should think of all these points when deciding whether a dance is right for a certain group. In addition, he should bear in mind that he may adapt a dance by eliminating complex actions and substituting others for them. The same dance may be presented in successive grades, each time with increasingly difficult steps. Those who cherish "authenticity" may object to this; they should realize that many different versions already exist for most of these dances and that by modifying a dance slightly the leader may make it possible for children to really enjoy it, rather than condemn them to frustration or not doing the dance at all. One should never pretend, of course, that such an adapted dance is completely authentic folk material.

## How to Teach Dances

In many ways the task of leading dances is similar to the job of the games leader, as described on pages 45 and 46.

The leader must prepare in advance a program geared for the abilities of the majority of children in the group. When leading any one dance, he asks the children to take the needed formation and then tells them what they are going to do. He may arouse interest by telling the background of the dance or by having its music played. Step by step, he demonstrates the action and has the children practice it to musical accompaniment. If he is using a phonograph (which makes it hard to play exactly the desired sequence of music), he may verbally give the rhythm and action commands. While teaching, he encourages the children at all times and helpfully corrects their mistakes. Then he puts the entire dance together and has the children practice it once more in the *same* musical tempo as the phonograph record or piano accompaniment. Finally they do the dance.

Creating an atmosphere of social ease and acceptance is important, particularly with children in the later elementary grades, when boy-girl mixing may meet some resistance. This difficulty is a reflection of the gang period, and is usually at its peak (if it appears at all) at about the sixth grade. It hinges on the boy's feeling that doing anything, particularly dancing, with girls, is sissy and to be avoided.

How should the adult leader deal with this temporary but touchy situation? First, he should not stress the idea of taking partners. Circle dances, line dances, or dances for threes are better than individual couple dances. Sometimes boys may be permitted at first to take partners with each other (provided they do not act up) and then gradually, when they have come to enjoy dancing more and more, asked to take partners with girls.

It is helpful to have men teachers or leaders assisting or actually directing the activity. Prestige may also be given to the dancing by having older groups (such as high school students) show favorite folk and square dances, or if this is not practical, showing films of adults enjoying folk and square dances. Special parties, play days, assembly programs, and other culminating events help to improve motivation.

The following section includes descriptions, with sheet music or record suggestions wherever possible, for a variety of dances and singing games that may be taught to six-to-twelve-year-olds. They are presented in the approximate order of their difficulty. However, leaders should certainly feel free to change this sequence in presenting them to a class or recreation group.

### SINGING GAMES

Most of the following games are generations old, and came to America from the British Isles and a few European countries. For the most part they are useful in the primary grades. Accompaniment may be provided by piano, accordion, guitar, banjo, or other simple instruments. However, the most important and suitable form of accompaniment comes from the voices of the children themselves; they should be helped to learn the songs and should be encouraged to sing out at all times as they do these games.

**How Do You Do, My Partner** (Swedish)

Folkraft Record 1190

[1] How do you do, my partner? How do you do today?
   Will you dance in the circle? I will show you the way.

[2] Tra-la-la-la-la-la, Tra-la-la-la-la-la,
   Tra-la-la-la-la-la,

[3] I will show you the way.

ACTION: [1] Children stand in a double circle, with partners facing. Boys are on the inside, girls on the outside. On the "How do you do" phrases, they shake hands with partners. On "Will you dance in the circle?" they join hands with partners. They slide counterclockwise around the circle during the chorus [2]. [3] Boys bow and girls curtsy to partners. After doing the dance a few times, they may learn to progress to new partners each time by moving one position to the left.

**Hickory Dickory Dock** (English)

Ruth Evans Record Series VII: "Nursery Rhymes and Singing Games"

[1] Hickory, dickory, dock, the mouse ran up the clock.

[2] The clock struck one, and down he'd run,

[3] Hickory, dickory, dock.

ACTION: [1] Standing in a single circle with hands joined, children stamp, left–right–left. They walk to the left. [2] They stop and each child claps his own hands on "one." They join hands and circle right. [3] They stop and stamp left–right–left on last "hickory, dickory, dock."

NOTE: There are many other possible actions for this rhyme; children should be encouraged to make up their own.

**Two Little Blackbirds** (English)

Ruth Evans Record Series VII: "Nursery Rhymes and Singing Games"

[1] Two little blackbirds, sitting on a hill,

[2] One named Jack, and the other named Jill.

[3] Fly away, Jack, and fly away, Jill.

[4] Come back, Jack, and come back, Jill.

ACTION: [1] Children stand in a double circle, facing partners. Boys stand on the inside, girls on the outside. On the word "sitting," each child kneels. [2] The boys spring up and clap hands on "Jack," and girls do the same on "Jill." [3] Each boy "flies away," waving his arms and traveling in a little circle away from his partner. Each girl does the same. [4] Each boy returns. Each girl returns.

**The Gallant Ship** (English)

[1] Three times around went our gallant ship, and three times around went she,

Three times around went our gallant ship, and she sank to the bottom of the sea.

[2] Haul her up! Haul her up! Came the word to the crew,

Haul her up! Haul her up! Cried they.

Haul her up! Haul her up! Came the word to the crew,

And they worked very hard that day.

ACTION: [1] Children stand in a double circle; outer circle walks clockwise, and inner circle counterclockwise. On the line "and she sank," children in the inner circle gradually sink to a deep knee bend as children in the outer circle face them. [2] Children in the outer circle pretend to be pulling ropes and turning windlasses, working hard. On the last line the "ships" rise.

**Jolly Is the Miller** (English)
Folkraft Record 1192

[1] Jolly is the miller who lives by the mill,
   The wheel goes around with a right good will.
[2] One hand in the hopper and the other in the sack,
[3] The right steps forward and the left steps back.

ACTION: [1] Children take partners and stand in a double circle, facing counterclockwise (Diagram 18). They march in this direction as one child

**Diagram 18**

in the center, the "miller," goes in the opposite direction. [2] As they keep marching, each child reaches out with his free hand and pretends to scoop the grain from the hopper and (with the same hand) to pour it into a sack in front of him. [3] Dropping partner's hand, each child in the double circle takes a new partner. (The child on the right steps forward, and the child on the left steps back one position). Meanwhile the "miller" tries to quickly steal another child as his partner. The game is repeated with a new "miller" or with the first "miller" trying again.

## Go Round and Round The Village (English)

Folkraft Record 1191

[1] Go 'round and 'round the village, [sing three times]
    As we have done before.
[2] Go in and out the windows, etc.
[3] Now stand and face a partner, etc.
[4] Now follow me to London, etc.

ACTION: [1] Children stand in a single circle, hands joined, facing in. Several other children skip or march around the outside of this circle. [2] Children in the circle raise joined hands to make arches as the "outer" children weave in and out under the arches. [3] The "outer" children choose partners and stand before them. [4] They join hands with them and skip counterclockwise around the inside of the circle while the others clap. When the game is played again, the original "outer" children join the circle and those they have chosen become the new "outer" children.

## I See You (Swedish)

Folkraft Record 1197

[1] I see you, I see you, tra-la-la-la-la-la.
    I see you, I see you, tra-la-la-la-la-la.
[2] You see me and I see you, you take me and I take you.
    You see me and I see you, you take me and I take you.

ACTION: [1] Two lines of boys face each other, each boy facing another boy directly, with about five feet between them. Behind each boy, with hands on his shoulders, is a girl (Diagram 19). Each girl bends her head slowly to the right, and then to the left, and then, faster, right, left, and right, playing peekaboo with the girl behind the opposite boy. The rhythm is: slow, slow, quick-quick-slow. This action is repeated: left, right, left-right-left. [2] Each girl claps her hands once and skips forward past her partner's left side. She joins both hands with the opposite girl, who has come out to meet her. They skip around four steps between the lines of boys. Each girl now claps hands and joins hands with her own partner (the boy). They skip around four steps in place. The dance ends with the girls now standing in lines facing each other and with each boy standing behind a girl. It is repeated from the beginning, with boys doing the action that the girls did the first time.

Diagram 19

**Bluebird** (American)
Folkraft Record 1180

[1] Bluebird, bluebird, in and out my window, [sing three times]
[2] Oh, Johnny, I am tired.
[3] Take a little girl and tap her on the shoulder, [sing three times]
     Oh, Johnny, I am tired.

ACTION: [1] All children but one stand facing in, in a single circle, hands joined high. One child, the Bluebird, walks in and out under the arches made by their arms, weaving his way around the circle. [2] He stands behind another child in the circle. (If he is a boy, he stands behind a girl, and vice versa.) [3] The Bluebird taps this child lightly with both hands on the shoulders. If a boy is being tapped, substitute the word "boy" in the verse. The game is repeated several times, with two, four, and then eight Bluebirds active, as new children are drawn into it.

### AMERICAN PLAY PARTIES

These lively mixers tend to be slightly more complicated than the singing games, not so much in terms of skills as in the fact that they usually have longer sequences. They may be introduced about the second or third grade, although a few, like "Sent My Brown Jug Downtown," are difficult enough for sixth graders. The best source for them is the *Handy Play-Party Book,* compiled by Lyn Rohrbough and published by the Cooperative Recreation Service, Delaware, Ohio. The words and melodies are usually so simple and catchy that children learn to sing them quickly and easily.

## Skip to My Lou
Folkraft Record 1192 or Folk Dancer Record 1110

[1] Skip, skip, skip to my Lou, [sing three times]
      Skip to my Lou, my darling.
[2] Lost my true love, what'll I do? etc.
[3] Found another one, prettier'n you, etc.

ACTION: [1] Children take partners (girl on the right, boy on the left) and walk or skip in a big circle, counterclockwise. [2] Each child drops his partner's hands. Girls continue to walk as in [1] while boys do an about-face and walk clockwise inside the circle of girls. [3] Each boy finds a new partner and does a two-hand skip-swing with her. If a youngster does not find a partner at once, he holds up his hand and goes into the center to look for one. The game is repeated several times from the beginning.

## Climbing up the Mountain
(Same music as "Skip to My Lou")
[1] Climbing up the mountain, two by two, [sing three times]
      Rise up, sugar, rise.
[2] Show us a little action, two by two, etc.
[3] That's a very fine action, two by two, etc.

ACTION: [1] Children take partners and, with hands joined in a single circle, walk left as one couple walks to the right inside the circle. [2] The outer circle stands still and claps as the inside couple demonstrates some action they have decided on while promenading. This may be any form of dance step, such as a swing, step-hop, skip, deep knee-bend, "patty-cake," elbow turn, polka, back-to-back slide, etc. [3] Each couple in the outer circle imitates this action as the inner couple continues to do it. At the end of the verse the inner couple picks a new couple to go into the center, to start the play party from the beginning while they go into the outer circle.

**Green Coffee**

[1] Green coffee grows on white oak trees,
   The rivers flow with brandy, Oh,
   Go choose you anyone you please,
   And swing like m'lasses candy, Oh.
[2] Somebody's rocking my sugar lump, [sing three times]
   Turn my sugar 'round, Oh.
[3] Just keep rocking my sugar lump, [sing three times]
   Turn my sugar 'round, Oh.

ACTION: [1] Children join hands in a single circle, facing in, without partners. This circle walks slowly to the right as one child, inside the circle, walks left. On "Go choose you . . ." he picks a partner of the opposite sex from the outside circle and brings her into the center. [2] The center couple does a skip-swing turning to the left (clockwise) as the outer circle slides rapidly to the right (counterclockwise) (Diagram 20). On "Turn my sugar 'round," those in the outer circle drop hands and turn so their backs are to the center. [3] The outer circle now slides right (clockwise) as the inner couple swings to the right (counterclockwise). On "Turn my sugar 'round" the outer circle turns to face the center and the first center player steps into the outer circle. The partner he selected starts the dance in the center from the beginning.

Diagram 20

**Four in a Boat**
Folk Dancer Record 1109

[1] Four in a boat and the tide rolls high, [sing three times]
  Get you a pretty one, bye and bye.
[2] Get me a pretty one, stay all day [sing three times]
  We don't care what the old folks say.
[3] Eight in the boat, and it won't go 'round, [sing three times]
  Swing that pretty one you've just found.
ACTION: [1] Children join hands in a single circle, facing in, without partners. Four boys stand in the center. The outer circle walks or skips counterclockwise; those inside go clockwise. On "Get you a pretty one," each boy
chooses a girl from the circle as his partner. [2] The outer circle continues
to the right as the couples in the center take promenade position and go
to the left (clockwise). [3] The outer circle stands still and claps while
those in the center swing. Then the boys go into the outer circle, and the
four girls start the dance in the center, from the beginning.

## Sent My Brown Jug Downtown

[1] Sent my brown jug downtown, [sing three times]
    So early in the morning.
[2] It came back with a waltz around, [sing three times]
    So early in the morning.
[3] Railroad, steamboat, river and canoe, [sing three times]
    Lost my true love, don't know what to do.
[4] Now she's gone, gone, gone, [sing three times]
    Now she's gone on that raging canoe.
[5] Let her go, go, go, [sing three times]
    Let her go on that raging canoe.

ACTION: [1] Couples join hands in a large single circle, taking partners (girl on boy's right) and circling to their left. [2] They circle back to the right. [3] Each child joins right hands with his partner and walks around her (Diagram 21A). He faces his corner (the child directly behind him in the circle), joins left hands with her, and walks around her. [4] He faces partner again. They join both hands, with arms extended out to the side (Diagram 21B). They take four slow sliding steps toward the center of the circle, at the same time rocking so their extended arms look like a windmill. On the last line of the verse they walk around each other clockwise, release hands, and walk past each other (passing right shoulders) toward their corners. **[5]** Joining hands with the corners, arms extended, they do four "windmill" steps as before, *away* from the center of the circle. On the last line each boy releases the girl's right hand but holds her left in his right. The girl turns out, so she is now on his right in the circle (they are both facing in toward the center), and they are ready to do the dance from the beginning with new partners.

Diagram 21A

Diagram 21B

**PLAY PARTIES IN LINE FORMATION**

**Old Brass Wagon** (TUNE: "Ten Little Indians"—American Folk Song)
Folk Dancer Record 1109

[1] Jumping up and down in the old brass wagon, [sing three times]
You're the one, my darling.

[2] Right and left in the old brass wagon, [sing three times]
You're the one, my darling.
One wheel off and t'other one draggin', [sing three times]
You're the one, my darling.

[3] We'll all run away with the old brass wagon, [sing three times]
You're the one, my darling.

ACTION: [1] Children stand in two lines, girls on one side facing boys on the other. There should be between four and six couples in each set. The first couple joins both hands and slides eight steps down between the lines,

Diagram 22

to the foot of the set, and then back up to place. **[2]** The first couple does a "reel." They join right elbows and turn around each other once in the center (Diagram 22). The boy then gives his left elbow to the next girl in line, turning around her, as the first girl does the same with the next boy in line, turning around her, as the first girl does the same with the next boy around. They repeat this, moving down the line, alternately turning with the next person in line with a left elbow, and with their partner with a right. They reel down to the foot of the set and stand at the end of their respective lines. Verse **[3]** is sung only if they need additional music to complete the action. The dance is repeated until every couple has completed the action.

**Jimmy Crack Corn** (Minstrel Song)
Folk Dancer Record 1111

**[1]** Jimmy crack corn, and I don't care, [sing three times]
      My master's gone away.
**[2]** Right hands up, etc.
**[3]** Left hands up, etc.
**[4]** Both hands up, etc.
**[5]** Roll 'em boys, etc. [this entire verse is repeated]

ACTION: **[1]** In line formation, as in "Old Brass Wagon," the first girl and last boy (diagonally opposite each other) take four steps toward each other, curtsy or bow, and take four steps back to place. The first boy and last girl do the same thing. This step may be a walk or skip. **[2]** The first girl and last boy go forward, join right hands, go around each other, and return to place. First boy and last girl repeat this. **[3]** Same action, with left hands. **[4]** Same action, with both hands. **[5]** All take partners in promenade position. The first couple leads the others in promenading to the left, down to the foot of the set, and back up to place again, without changing the order of the couples. The first couple goes down under an arch formed by the joined hands of the other couples, to the foot of the set. A new couple begins the dance from **[1]** and it is continued until every couple has been active.

## NATIONAL FOLK DANCES

**Green Sleeves** (English)
RCA Victor Record 45–6175

FORMATION: Couples face to the right, in a double circle, each girl on her partner's right. One couple stands directly behind another, and there are spaces between the groups of two couples.

ACTION: **[1]** All march sixteen lively steps forward (counterclockwise), holding partner's inside hand (Diagram 23A). **[2]** The leading couple in each group of two couples turns back, the boy turning to his right and the girl to her left. They join right hands with the couple behind and walk

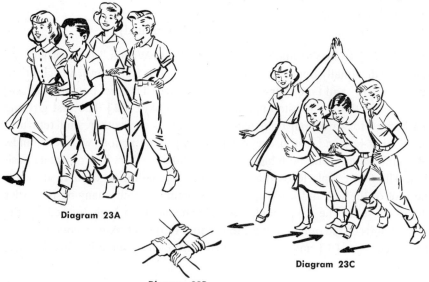

**Diagram 23A**

**Diagram 23C**

**Diagram 23B**

eight steps clockwise in a right-hand star (Diagram 23B). They turn, put left hands in, and walk eight steps counterclockwise in a left-hand star. They then face forward in the starting position. **[3]** The last action is called, "turning the sleeves." The leading couple, still facing forward, bends over slightly and walks backward *under* an arch formed by the joined, raised hands of the rear couple, which walks forward (Diagram 23C). The action is reversed; the couple that had just gone under the arch now raises an arch and walks forward while the other couple backs under. This entire step is repeated. The dance is then repeated several times from the beginning.

**Kinderpolka** (German)

RCA Victor Record 45–6179

FORMATION: Children stand in a single circle, facing partners. Boys face counterclockwise; girls face clockwise.

ACTION: **[1]** Children join hands with their partners, arms extended out to the sides. Each couple takes two slow slide steps toward the center of the circle. They then stamp three times (the boy stamps, left–right–left, and the girl stamps, right–left–right). They take two slow slide steps away from the center of the circle and stamp three times (boy: right–left–right, girl: left–right–left). This entire action is repeated. **[2]** Each child claps his hands against his knees (or lower thighs), then claps his hands together, then against his partner's hands, three times. This entire action is repeated. **[3]** Each child springs so his right foot is forward, heel on the floor, toe up (weight is on the left foot). At the same time, he shakes his right index finger at his partner three times, holding right elbow in left hand. Then he springs so his left foot is forward and he shakes his left index finger. Each child turns around in place and stamps three times. The entire dance is repeated several times from the beginning.

**Crested Hen** (Danish)
RCA Victor Record 45–6176

FORMATION: Children join hands in small circles of three, with one boy and two girls, or vice versa (Diagram 24A).

ACTION: **[1]** All do eight step-hops to the left, and then back to the right. **[2]** The two children of the same sex release each other's hand so they are standing in a line of three, with the odd child between the other two. The center child forms an arch with the child on his left by raising their joined hands. The child on the right goes forward, under this arch, and back to place, with four step-hops (Diagram 24B). Still holding hands, the center

Diagram 24A

Diagram 24B

child turns to the left under the arch as this child goes through, so all are now facing forward again. The center child now forms an arch with the child on his right. The left-hand child step-hops forward, under this arch, and back to place as the center child turns under the arch, to his right. All are facing forward again. This entire action [2] is repeated. The dance is then repeated from the beginning.

**Good Humor** (English)

World of Fun Record M-109A (Methodist Publishing House)

FORMATION: Couples stand in a single circle, facing in, hands joined.

ACTION: [1] All take four steps forward and backward, twice. All the girls take four steps forward, clapping hands on the last step, and four steps back to place. All the boys do the same. [2] All turn to face corners (boys face left; girls face right). All swing corners for sixteen counts (younger children may do a two-hand skipping swing; older children take regular dance position and do a "buzz swing" as in square dancing). [3] Each boy takes this girl as his new partner; they face to the right and promenade counterclockwise for sixteen steps. They face the center and begin the dance again, with this girl on the boy's right.

**Ace of Diamonds** (Danish)

RCA Victor Record 45–6169

FORMATION: Couples in a double circle; boys facing out, girls facing in.

ACTION: [1] Each child claps hands and links right elbows with his partner; they run once around each other and return to place. They clap hands again, link left elbows, and run around each other again. [2] With hands placed on hips, each child springs so his right foot is forward, heel on floor, toe up. Then he springs so the left is forward. Then, faster, he places right, left and right, forward. This entire action is repeated, starting with the left foot. The count is: right, left, right–left–right. Left, right, left–right–left. [3] They do a polka for the remainder of the dance (eight polka steps). Young children may simply join hands in promenade position and skip around the floor during this part of the music. Older children may do the polka step forward in promenade position *without* turning. As a final phase of the progression, children who have learned to do the turning polka step correctly may do it in closed couple position.

## American Square Dances

There are many square dances which are suitable for children in elementary school, beginning at about the third or fourth grade, provided that the basic action, or "figure," and the accessory actions, or "trimmings," are kept fairly simple.

In presenting any square dance, the leader must teach it first by demonstrating the action and having the children walk through it. Then he calls it himself (using piano music or a record for accompaniment), or he plays a record which has both music and calls on it. If he does the calling himself, which is always preferable, in the author's opinion, the leader should emphasize the rhythmic beat and make all his directions loud, clear, and enthusiastic. Particularly the important directional calls, such as "swing" or "circle left," should be stressed.

There are two chief types of square dance calls: "singing" and "patter." The "singing" call is fitted exactly, and sung to a particular melody. The "patter" call is chanted rhythmically against the background of a hoedown tune, and does not attempt to follow the melodic line. Since calling is a definite skill which the leader must acquire, it is helpful for him to attend square dances, to learn suitable dances and calls, and to get the general hang of how to do it. Four good examples of square dances for children follow; there are many additional dances in the author's two books: *Square Dances of Today,* and *Recreation Leader's Handbook,* and in the RCA Victor "Let's Square Dance" series, Albums 1 and 2 (3000 and 3001), with calls and directions by Richard Kraus.

## Description of Basic Square Dance Terms

*Formation.* Each square dance set (Diagram 25) has four couples, one on each side of the square, facing in. Each girl is on her partner's right. The first couple stands with its back to the leader or to the music; the others are numbered counterclockwise "two," "three" and "four." The boy on a girl's right is her "corner." Thus the first boy and fourth girl are corners. The first girl and second boy are corners. The first and third couples are "head" couples. The second and fourth are "side" couples.

*Basic Step.* The basic movement in square dancing for adults is a light, graceful walking step. Children, however, like to do a skip; provided that they keep it under control, they should be permitted to do it.

*Swing.* Young children may join both hands with their partners and skip around, turning clockwise. Older children, in fifth or sixth grades, may learn to swing the adult way, with a "buzz swing," in which they take a position similar to ballroom dancing, but with the right shoulders slightly turned toward each other. They place right feet forward and pivot on them, while pushing with rapid short steps with left feet (as on a scooter).

*Allemande Left.* Each child faces his corner. He joins left hands with the corner, walks around her, and back to place, facing his partner.

*Grand Right and Left.* This usually follows the "allemande left." It is a chaining or weaving action, in which the boys go counterclockwise and the girls clockwise around the square. It begins by giving right hands to partners and walking past them (passing right shoulders). Children give left hands to the next person and pass them by the left shoulder. This is continued until they meet their partners on the opposite side of the square. They take them in promenade position and walk counterclockwise back to place.

Other basic actions will be described in the dances in which they appear.

**SINGING SQUARE DANCES**

**Hinkey Dinkey Parlez Vous**
Folkraft Record F-1220B

CALLS:

[1] Allemande left your corners all, parlez vous,
   Grand chain eight around the hall, two by two,
   Meet your partner, what do you do?
   Promenade home, that's what you do, Hinkey, Dinkey, Parlez Vous!

[2] Head two girls go forward and back, parlez vous,
   The same two girls, you do-si-do, parlez vous,
   Do-si-do your corners all, do-si-do your partners all,
   Hinkey, Dinkey, Parlez Vous!

[3] Swing your partners round and round, parlez vous,
   Promenade around the town, two by two,
   Promenade eight, promenade all,
   Places all and hear my call, Hinkey, Dinkey, Parlez Vous!

ACTION: [1] All dancers face their corners, give left hands to them, and walk around them. They give right hands to their partners and do a grand right and left (see page 112). They meet partners and promenade home. [2] The head two girls (one and three) walk four steps forward, curtsy, and back four steps to place. They go forward again and do-si-do passing right shoulders and return to place. All dancers do-si-do their corners and then their partners. [3] All swing partners and promenade them home. The side girls (two and four) then do actions [2] and [3]. Then all do the allemande left and grand right and left again. Actions [2] and [3] are repeated, with the head two boys and then the side two boys active. End with the allemande left and grand right and left.

**Hot Time in the Old Town**
Windsor Record 7115-B

CALLS:

**[1]** Allemande left to the corner you will go,
Grand right and left, around the outside row.
Meet your partner, and promenade her home,
There'll be a hot time in the old town tonight!

**[2]** All four girls, to the center of the ring,
All four boys, promenade around the ring.
Pass your partner, the next one you will swing,
There'll be a hot time in the old town tonight.

ACTION: **[1]** Allemande left and grand right and left as in previous direc-

Diagram 26

tions. [2] All four girls walk to the center and stand there back to back, facing their home positions. Boys walk around the outside of the set to the right (Diagram 26). Each boy goes completely around, then passes his partner and swings the next girl. This action [2] is repeated three times more; each boy swings a new girl every time until he has his partner back. Then all do the allemande left and grand right and left [1] again. Action [2] is repeated, but with the boys going to the center and the girls walking around the outside (the calls are changed accordingly). End with action [1].

### PATTER SQUARE DANCES

The previous squares included allemande left calls since they were singing squares. In the following patter-style dances only the calls and descriptions for the basic figures are given. Therefore, it is up to the caller to add "opening," "break," and "closing" calls. Here are sample calls he can use:

OPENING CALLS: All join hands and circle south,
Let a little moonshine in your mouth,
You're all going wrong, go back the other way,
Hold your holts and re-sashay.

BREAK CALLS: Allemande left to your left hand,
Right to your partner for a right and left grand,
Meet your partner, pretty little thing,
And all promenade around the ring.

CLOSING CALLS: Promenade your partner off the floor,
That's all there is, there is no more.

By placing the opening calls at the introduction of the dance, the break calls at points in the square after units of action have been completed, and the closing calls at the end, the leader can use the following figures to construct complete patter square dances. Both the following patter-style dances can be done to the music of "Little Brown Jug," RCA Victor Album 3000.

### Duck for the Oyster

CALLS:

[1] First couple out to the couple on the right,

Circle four for half the night.

Duck for the oyster, duck, Dive for the clam, dive!

Duck on through, and go to the next.

ACTION: [1] The first couple walks to the second and joins hands with them. They circle left halfway so the first couple is facing the center of the set. Continuing to hold hands, the second couple raises their joined hands in an arch. The first couple ducks halfway under this arch and back (Diagram 27). Now the first couple makes the arch and the second couple

Diagram 27

ducks under and back. The second couple makes the arch and the first couple ducks completely through. The first couple goes to the third couple and does this entire action with them, then on to the fourth, and back to their home position. Each couple leads out to do the action in turn. Opening, break, and closing calls listed on page 115 should be added to this.

### Take a Little Peek

CALLS:

[1] First couple out to the couple on the right,
Go around that couple, take a little peek.
Back to the center, swing your sweet.
Go around that couple, peek once more.
Back to the center, swing all four.

ACTION: [1] The first couple walks to, and faces, the second. The first couple separates (boy to left, girl to right); they lean over and "peek" around the second couple (Diagram 28), then return to the center and swing. The first couple repeats this action and then both couples swing. The first couple does the same action with the third and then the fourth couples. Each couple leads out to do the action in turn. Additional opening, break, and closing calls should be added where suitable.

Diagram 28

## Basic Ballroom Dance Steps

Many children in the years just preceding adolescence (fifth and sixth grades) learn to do ballroom dancing in private classes, in classes sponsored by Parent-Teacher Associations, or from parents or older brothers and sisters. Since this kind of dancing will become very important to them shortly at parties and school dances, it is wise to give them enough skill so that they will feel confidence and ease on the dance floor. A broad repertoire including the latest dance crazes is not essential, but they should be able to do a box step and forward or backward step in waltz and fox-trot rhythms.

Teaching ballroom dancing to children of this age is somewhat difficult because many of them have not yet perfected rhythmic and neuromuscular skills that are required—and also because they are likely to resist partner-taking. Recognizing this, it is a good idea not to attempt to stress polished dance movement, but to strive for accurate movement to rhythm and a broad understanding of the basic steps.

In teaching it is helpful to have all the children stand in a "block" formation facing the same side of the room while they practice any given step. Thus they can watch and pick up the actions from those around them (since they should all be moving in the same way). From this formation the teacher may then have them take lines, with boys facing girls, to practice the actions that are different for each sex. Only when they have thoroughly mastered a step should they be put into couples, and it is helpful to have partners rotated frequently to minimize the objections that some youngsters will raise. In fact dancing with partners should not take more than about one-third of any ballroom dance session with preteens (until they are quite experienced). The remaining time may be devoted to practicing various rhythms, teaching them as individuals, and even folk or square dancing—to keep the atmosphere lively and informal.

The author has had greatest success with children in beginning with the box step of the fox trot.

### FOX TROT

*Box Step.* Children should practice: [1] stepping forward with the left foot, placing weight on it; [2] placing the right foot forward and out to the side, placing weight on it; [3] placing the left foot next to the right with weight on it; [4] stepping back with the right foot, placing weight on it; [5] stepping back and to the side with left foot; [6] placing the right foot next to the left.

This action is practiced to fox-trot rhythm. Children should first listen to very simple and clear fox-trot music, which they should practice clapping to. The beat is: *One*-two-three-four, *One*-two-three-four, etc., with the first count of each measure emphasized. Then the box step is fitted to the fox-trot rhythm:

| MUSICAL COUNT | DANCE ACTION (Diagram 29A). |
|---|---|
| *One* | Step forward with the left foot. |
| Two | Begin to bring right foot forward. |
| Three | Place right foot on floor. |
| Four | Place left foot next to right. |
| | |
| *One* | Step back on right foot (Diagram 29B). |
| Two | Begin to bring left foot back. |
| Three | Place weight on left foot. |
| Four | Place right foot next to left. |

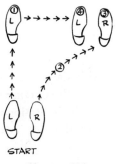

Diagram 29A

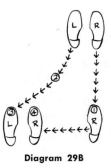

Diagram 29B

When children have practiced this individually and know it fairly well, they should take partners and do it. When the boy begins by stepping forward on the left foot, the girl steps back on the right foot.

*Forward Step.* This is similar to the box step except that it is done moving steadily in one direction. Children [1] step forward with the left foot, [2] step forward and to the side with the right foot, and [3] place the left foot next to the right. Then they [4] step forward with the right foot, [5] step forward and to the side with the left foot, and [6] place the right foot next to the left. In rhythm, this becomes:

| MUSICAL COUNT | DANCE ACTION |
|---|---|
| *One* | Step forward with left. |
| Two | Begin to bring right forward. |
| Three | Place right on floor. |
| Four | Place left next to right. |
| *One* | Step forward with right. |
| Two | Begin to bring left forward. |
| Three | Place left on floor. |
| Four | Place right next to left. |

When children have learned this individually, they do it with partners. The boy starts by moving forward with his left foot, and the girl by going back with her right. He keeps going forward and she keeps going backward. When they have thoroughly learned the box step and forward step, they may combine them by doing two complete box steps and four forward steps in a continuing combination.

### WALTZ

The basic ballroom waltz may be done with the same steps as the fox trot except that the rhythmic count is: *One,* two, three; *One,* two, three. This speeds up the action somewhat and eliminates the hesitation that comes on the second count of the fox trot. In waltz rhythm the box step and forward step become:

| MUSICAL COUNT | BOX STEP ACTION | FORWARD STEP |
|---|---|---|
| *One* | Step forward with left foot. | Step forward with left foot. |
| Two | Place right foot forward and to side. | Place right foot forward and to side. |
| Three | Place left next to right. | Place left next to right. |

| | | |
|---|---|---|
| *One* | Step backward with right foot. | Step forward with right foot. |
| Two | Place left foot backward and to side. | Place left foot forward and to side. |
| Three | Place right next to left. | Place right next to left. |

Before introducing a new rhythm such as waltz it is wise to help the children become accustomed to moving to it in different ways, such as clapping, swinging, turning, walking, playing rhythm instruments, or stamping or moving other parts of their bodies. When they are actually doing the steps to music, it helps them to have the leader call out rhythmical directions such as "*Forward,* side, together; *backward,* side, together."

## Summary

This chapter has presented leadership techniques and suitable materials in the following forms of traditional dancing: singing games and play parties, folk, square, and ballroom dancing. The following chapter outlines additional methods and materials in the area of creative rhythms and dance movement.

# CHAPTER 8

# CREATIVE RHYTHMS

The creative approach to dance places the stress on enriching each child's total personality by encouraging self-expression and developing essential skills and appreciations in the areas of music, rhythm, and bodily movement.

There are a variety of basic leadership approaches which may be used. Some adult leaders will attempt to develop completely free and unguided movement based solely on the child's spontaneous reaction to music or percussive accompaniment. Such a leader will offer no direction, suggestion, or teaching hint that might shape the child's response. Other adults may develop a series of learning situations, problems, and experiences and will systematically drill children in specific techniques which are very much like those offered in adult modern-dance classes.

Most leaders—whether they are working in schools or recreational settings—are likely to fall between these two extremes. Obviously each leader must use the approach that he has confidence in and that he feels is likely to bring about desired objectives in terms of children's growth.

## Objectives of Creative Rhythms

*Emotionally Freeing the Child.* Many young children are likely to be troubled and inhibited emotionally, either by challenges in the school or playground situation or as a result of family relationships. Through dance experience, in which they can move freely, fully, and beautifully, they discover a wonderful means of freeing the spirit, releasing inner drives, and relaxing tensions and anxiety.

A graduate student in one of the author's classes who had been a

122

music teacher in a Texas school system wrote of Lili, a Mexican-American child: [33]

Lili was . . . over-age for her grade but too young to be allowed to quit school. She attended as seldom as possible, always in the company of her younger sister, her only companion. . . . Lili's hair was never combed, her face never washed and her dress usually dirty. The children openly made fun of her and called her "Lili Goose," a name she disliked immensely and which sent her in rapid pursuit of any offender. I had Lili twice a week in music class and her voice had been so abused that when she tried to sing, it was as ugly and harsh as when she spoke. Lili was also a discipline problem in the entire school system . . . I often hoped that she would be absent. . . .

. . . during the last few months of school, my younger children began to make up a few elementary Indian dances which became quite a craze. One of the dances we called the "Thunderbird Dance" and as accompaniment I played a lovely melody on the piano which had a strong basic Spanish rhythm. One day the older girls asked if they might not be allowed to march and then try to do a few Indian steps like their little brothers and sisters were doing . . . soon they were all marching around the room. One by one the girls became tired and took their seats. When I finally came to the Spanish rhythm, everyone was in her seat except Lili. Lili was at the front of the room making up her own dance. All eyes were on her but she was too busy to notice. Her arms and body swayed to and fro as she improvised steps right and left and back and around. When the music was completed, the whole room broke into applause.

"Lili," I said, "Why didn't you tell me you could dance?"

There was no answer, just a big, happy smile.

"Let Lili dance again," someone said. "Yes," cried others, "Let Lili dance again." "Are you too tired to dance some more, Lili?" I asked. No, Lili was not too tired, and Lili danced again.

At the end of the class, I asked Lili if I would occasionally send for her during school and it was all right with her other teachers, would she come and demonstrate for some of the other music classes? She gladly consented.

Next morning before school, Lili came by my room in a pretty, clean dress, her hair combed and her face washed. "Don't forget to send for me," she called.

Lili was asked many times to come to classes. Her conduct improved, and her appearance and adjustment to school as well. The children soon forgot "Lili Goose." She became "Lili, the dancer." Often after that, when Lili came to perform for a group of younger children, I would ask them, just to please her, "What was the first thing you said when you came into the room today?"

"Let Lili dance," they would shout.

I sincerely believe that so many seemingly serious problems in our schools today could be easily overcome if we knew how and occasionally would just "Let Lili dance."

*Developing Creative Expression.* What is creativity? It is the inner child speaking truthfully, not producing an object or action that he feels is desired by the adult leader or that adheres to standards imposed on him.

Through bodily movement, which is the most direct, powerful, and primitive means of self-expression, each youngster can freely communicate his innermost feelings of beauty, fear, love, anger, humor, or sadness. Any other medium demands its special tools and instruments: painting requires brush, paint, and canvas; formal music requires instruments and technique; even speech demands verbal skills and vocabulary. The urge to express oneself through meaningful gesture and attitude is as old as mankind and resides in all of us today. In addition, the fact that, from earliest babyhood, the child is aware of rhythm as a life force, in his own body, his surroundings, and in the universe itself, makes rhythm an ideal medium of creative expression.

In dance children are able to evoke ideas, sentiments, and attitudes showing their feelings about all of the elements and forces in their lives— physical and spiritual. As they do this, they also learn to judge what is true and good in art and to perceive elements of beauty in all forms of life. They grow to appreciate sincerity and honesty of expression, which will help them build a mature conception of living artistically and creatively in all phases of later life.

*Skills.* At the same time the child is given continuing opportunities to develop basic skills and understandings in the realms of music appreciation and performance and physical movement. He becomes familiar with technical elements of music and rhythm, becomes sensitive to the different qualities of musical sound, and learns to use simple instruments to make music and rhythm. Simultaneously he is given experience in a wide variety of movement skills; gradually these skills are sharpened and he gains the confidence that comes from knowing the "why" and "how" of what he is doing.

While younger children may be satisfied to respond to musical stimuli in an undisciplined, naïve fashion (which is no less worthy for being so and is suited to their stage of growth) older children appreciate training and guidance that will help them move more efficiently and meaningfully. Such training does not eliminate creativity. On the contrary, it simply means that, when new possibilities for movement are opened up to the child by having him become aware of concepts of space, design, levels, direction, and focus, and when his body has become strong and limber, his range of self-expression has become much greater. He has been given improved tools for self-expression, but the expression remains his own.

One teacher has described it thus: [34]

> In our classes our first aim is to define and establish the natural balance and alignment of the body so that the pupil may attain a beautiful, free and strong use of movement. Our second aim, through the use of rhythm, improvisation, imaginative image and simple dance steps and patterns, is to give the student an experience of dance as an art form.
>
> The young child, generally up to the age of seven, should not be forced into techniques, but should develop coordination, the ability to listen to music and to move rhythmically through imaginative idea and dramatic play. From the age of eight on the child is muscularly and psychologically ready for a progressively more conscious approach to dance which includes both ballet and modern dance techniques. However, as often as possible the teacher uses a dramatic image to give the simplest exercise or problem an inner motivation.

## The Leader's Approach

Each leader must develop his own method of working with creative rhythms based on his own philosophy of education or play leadership and his personal skills and areas of competence. There is no cut-and-dried, infallible method. This chapter, rather than outline a single sequence of activities, will offer a broad approach including a variety of useful devices for stimulating creative movement, skills, and understanding. Each leader may use these as he sees fit; in many cases they will serve as take-off points for new kinds of ventures. Children will have many ideas to contribute and through their enthusiasm and suggestions will shape the course of the continuing experience.

Certain general principles apply:

The leader must be resourceful and persistent in drawing out and encouraging individual self-expression, rather than stereotyped responses.

Praise and encouragement are needed at all times; the child must never feel that his expression might not be accepted.

The leader should realize that he need not possess a high level of personal skills to be effective in this area, although music and dance training is obviously helpful.

No rigid timetable or chart of expectations can be set up. The process of creative growth is often slow, disorganized, and disappointing when compared with the results of "taught" activity.

The rhythmic experience should be integrated, as much as possible, with the child's surroundings and other play or school activities. Creative dance is closely linked to musical expression, dramatic play, the language arts, and the graphic arts. All are concerned with the child's reaction to, and interpretation of, the world around him.

## Beginning Rhythms

Children begin to move rhythmically long before they come into contact with adult leaders as such. During the latter part of the first year, and increasingly in the second year, they move freely and spontaneously to music (radio, television, records, or mother's singing) and enjoy beating out their own rhythms with toy drums or battered kitchen utensils. When their footing becomes fairly secure, they may be encouraged to dance by themselves or side by side with other children. At first the action is likely to be a simple, erratic run or a stamping or arm-waving in place. Gradually children who have been encouraged or who have the opportunity to watch dancing on television or in real life are likely to show a greater variety of steps and movements—kicks, turns, leaps, and whirls. As they become more aware of the different qualities of music, they may also move in different tempos or show different levels of excitement, according to the mood of the music.

All this should be encouraged as part of early growth, although no effort should be made to direct the play or teach specific actions.

During the nursery school and kindergarten period, such play should be continued with the increasing accompaniment of children's records and singing on the part of the child and adult leader. Occasionally action songs or nursery rhymes which make use of limited pantomimic movements (usually hand actions) may be used. These are fun and encourage expressive movement. However, the idea should not be stressed that set actions must accompany every song or that every such play-song must be done in a certain way. Certainly, it is sometimes fun for children all to be doing the same thing at the same time.

Gradually children at four and five may also be introduced to such traditional games as London Bridge, Farmer in the Dell, Looby Loo, and Mulberry Bush. They do these in a fragmentary, stop-and-go way because they are not yet capable of understanding group organization and do not really want to fit into a complicated experience. But they enjoy following the leader in various actions or walking around in a circle to music or forming simple arches or even taking partners. No effort should be made to polish such games at an early age; by the time they are six or seven, children are able to play and sing them correctly—that is, as they are written in the books or played on records.

At the same time children should have plenty of continuing opportunity to move freely to music (piano, record, or other accompaniment). There should be no conscious teaching of skills or guidance of movements during such sessions and no effort to pin down "meanings" to the dance action.

## Movement Skills

During the primary grades it is customary for some of the dance activity to be devoted to learning and practicing a wide variety of movement skills such as walking, running, skipping, hopping, jumping, galloping, sliding, swinging, bending, turning, and bouncing. Suitable music for accompanying these actions has been prepared by Deborah Hunt Jennings.

Among the most useful phonograph records for rhythmic accompaniment are:

"Childhood Rhythms," Albums I, II, III, and IV, published by Ruth Evans, 326 Forest Park Ave., Springfield, Mass.

"Music for Rhythms and Dance," published by Freda Miller, 8 Tudor City Place, New York, N.Y.

The Evans records are very simple musically and offer a very clear rhythmic beat, while the Miller records are more complex and, at the same time, more stimulating.

To begin, the teacher may simply play the music and ask the children to move about the floor as they wish. If the rhythm is clear, it is likely that a majority of the youngsters will move in a way that fits the music well—no matter what the suggested action for the record is. A few children who lack ideas for movement or are unsure of themselves will probably look about them and copy what the others are doing.

**WALKING**

**RUNNING**

**SKIPPING**

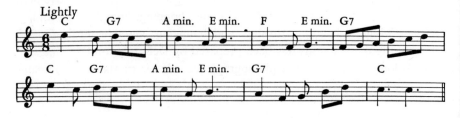

**MARCHING**

**SWINGING**

**STRIKING**

If for some reason children cannot seem to work out a movement that fits the rhythm well, the teacher might play the music, ask the children to listen, and then ask for volunteers to show how they might move to it. After several individuals had shown what they would do, the entire group might be asked to move to the music, picking any of the actions that have been shown.

Sometimes, if the leader wants to have the children learn a specific action, she may lead the group herself as the music plays or have them practice it before the music is played. But more often it is best to have the ideas come from the children themselves. Sometimes this can be done through listening and discussion:

"It's very fast—let's run to it."

"I feel like bouncing like a rubber ball."

"Joe, you take Mary's hand and skip with us across the room."

"Very quiet. Just tiptoe. Shhhh. . ."

"I'm drooping, dropping, flopping, flapping, just like a rag doll. No bones. Just a rag doll. . ."

*Types of Movements.* There are two chief types of movements which are practiced in such sessions: "locomotor" movements (which involve traveling around the floor) and "axial," or body, movements (which are usually done in one place or with very little traveling).

*Locomotor Movements.* These include walking, running, hopping (on one foot), jumping (on two feet), leaping, skipping (walk and hop), galloping (walk and leap, moving forward, with one foot continuing to lead), sliding (walk and leap, to the side), and, in time, more complicated skills, such as the polka, schottische, and mazurka.

*Axial Movements.* These actions include bending, swinging, pushing, turning, bouncing, pulling, stretching, dodging, striking, and similar movements.

As children gain skill in these actions, they may be urged to put them together in combinations such as run and bend, dodge and hop, jump and slide, push and shake, etc. A number of records have been made which offer accompaniment for this type of exercise, or the teacher may improvise accompaniment with a drum.

In addition to learning the various rhythmic movements, children should gradually become aware of the ways in which they can use the actions. In discussion, through demonstration, or through watching other children, they realize that there are many possibilities.

*Levels.* "We can be very high, very low, or anywhere in between. A whole group of us can be on tiptoes, stretching up. Some can crawl on their stomachs. Others can run low. Or we can have different kinds of music. When we hear the tambourines, we can go high. When we hear the big drum, we can go low."

*Direction.* "We started going around in a circle, all together. That's good for traffic—but we can go any way we want to. We can move forward, backward, or sideways. We can move up and down. We can go in a diagonal line—part forward and part to the side. We can turn as we go. We can look one way and move another."

*Range of Movement.* "We can make tiny little movements with just one part of the body, when you play the music quietly. We can take great big movements—jumping with our whole body—when we hear something else. We can move two parts of our bodies at once, or more."

*Quality of Movement.* "We can move all different ways. Sometimes we can be very smooth, just like molasses running out of a jug. Sometimes we can be very rough and jerky, like an old car going over a bad road. If you give us different noises, like a door creaking open, or rain falling on a roof, we can move the way that makes us feel."

*Space.* "We can fill up the space of the room with our movements in all kinds of ways. We can move around in circles or squares or triangles or even spirals. We can draw a design on the blackboard or on newsprint and then move that way. We can draw an animal or a number or a letter of the alphabet and then make that kind of a design with our movement on the floor."

*Partners.* "We can move all by ourselves or we can dance with somebody else. Sometimes we can be in threes or fours or more. We can hold hands in a little circle or we can stand in a line with hands on shoulders. There are lots of ways we can dance with each other."

## Pantomimic Play

At the same time that children explore movements that have no literal meaning, they also take great delight in "acting things out" through movement. They love to be elephants (slow and heavy, with the trunk swinging), lions (snarling, crawling up, then leaping and clawing), and horses (lively galloping across the field). They quickly see the possibilities in all sorts of animals, toys, mechanical objects, and vehicles—in jumping jacks, circus clowns, airplanes, trains, boats, buzz-saws, and swings. They can become anything that has a characteristic movement, rhythm, shape, or sound and is part of their world of interest.

Sometimes they may show actions to other children without any accompaniment.

"This is an elevator. Going up! Third floor—ladies' coats!"

Or: "Guess what I am now. We saw one yesterday."

Specific actions may be suggested by the leader more or less directly. She might say, "Here's some music. What is this drawing on the record cover? A kangaroo, Jimmy? Let's play it. You listen—and then show me how you think a kangaroo might move." Or the music might be played, with each child urged to move to it as he pleased. Then the youngsters might talk about the different animals they wanted to be while it was playing and they might all decide to be one thing at a time.

Some records, such as Saint-Saens' "Carnival of the Animals," give music for different animals without verbally labeling them. Others, like the Ruth Evans Series or the RCA Victor records, give specific titles for each band of music. The leader and children may make use of these suggestions or not, as they please. Often records have voices on them giving specific suggestions for action; when this is the case, children usually respond to the ideas offered, although they may interpret them quite differently. An example is the Young People's Record, "Winter Fun."

> Lift your feet high in the deep snow,
> In the soft snow, smooth and white.
> High steps, way up, deep steps, way down,
> In the clean snow, cold and bright.

Or:

> Pushing, pushing, pushing snow-plow, push aside the snow.
> Turn around for another load—little snow-plow, clear the road.

Or:

> Come skate with me, over the ice;
> Come and I'll show you, to skate is nice.
> Skate on your left, skate on your right,
> Skate in the sunshine, flashing bright.

Many record companies issue records like this designed to stimulate creative, dramatic expression. Some are quite hackneyed and mechanical or, because of their rapid succession of different images, unsuited for rhythmic participation. Others are excellent for the purpose and may be used again and again, with children constantly adding to their interpretations and ideas.

Often the use of such records may be made more successful by first discussing the subject matter involved. Children may listen to songs and poems about the activity or may make up their own songs and poems. Following a trip or a film-showing they may draw pictures based on it, listen to music that suggests the action, and finally dance their reactions, either individually or in a more organized way.

One example is the circus. After going to a circus or even after seeing a circus show on television, children may talk about all the things they saw and enjoyed—the animals in the sideshow, the tightrope walker, the trapeze artists, the bareback riders, and the lion tamer. To develop ideas further they may draw pictures of the circus and put them on the wall. Then, to a lively record which suggests a spirit of celebration and joyous activity but gives no specific images, they may dance any of the roles that have been mentioned or that they remember—or dance in a completely free way based on the spirit of the circus. The leader may then ask half the children to dance while the others watch, and then reverse the procedure so each child can see the variety of ideas and possibilities. Children might talk about the ideas or actions they liked best and might form small groups to perform each action—possibly with the addition of special accompaniment by suitable rhythm instruments. They may even choose a ringmaster who will introduce each act with a flourish, and thus have their own classroom or play group circus.

*Choral Speaking.* Speech, by itself or accompanied by a percussive beat, may be used to stimulate pantomimic dance movement or rhythmic play. There are many possibilities in collections of children's verse, and youngsters themselves may easily make up their own verses for this purpose. The following examples show how, if the italicized syllable is emphasized, definite meters or qualities of movement can be achieved:

*Skip*ping is *fun, skip*ping is *fun, skip*ping is *fun* for *every*one,
The *more* you skip, the *bet*ter you skip, so *skip, skip, skip.*

Or:

*El*ephants *walk,* like *this,* like *that,*
They're *ter*ribly *big* and *ter*ribly *fat,*
They *have* no *hands,* they *have* no *toes,*
But *good*ness *gra*cious, *what* a *nose.*

*Integration with Other Subjects.* Throughout all such activities the teacher or leader should try to encourage individual expression and unique and original movements that capture the spirit of whatever the theme is. Where possible such themes should be related to other learning or recreational experiences of the children. If third-grade youngsters are learning about farm life, many of the day-by-day tasks of rural living may be dealt with in a mimetic way. If they are studying "Transportation" as a unit, they might talk about, draw, and "dance out" such ideas as "Traffic Policeman on a corner, signaling cars, trucks, bicycles, and pedestrians to go by." (Particularly good music for this is George Gershwin's "American in Paris.")

Famous events from history may be "danced out" or when children are learning about peoples of other lands, many ideas for creative movement are likely to occur to them. Such expressions may be combined with folk dances and songs at United Nations celebrations or international play days or festivals.

*Prestructured Mimetic Materials.* In older collections of children's dances and rhythms there often appear cut and dried mimetic materials with specific action suggested, fitted exactly to music that has been prepared for the purpose. Such a dance or exercise might be titled "The Brownies and the Evil Fairy" and might read like this:

Measures 1–4     The Brownies run out into a field and pick flowers
Measures 5–8     They join hands in a circle and skip clockwise
Measures 9–12     The Evil Fairy, who has been hiding behind a tree, creeps up to surprise them

Because they fail to truly stimulate children's imaginations or provide for creative growth, such activities are, for the most part, considered to be outmoded today. However, for the teacher or play leader lacking confidence in this field they may appear to offer a desirable "crutch" to lean on.

*"Mood Projection."* A final form of acting out is that of "mood projection," in which children do not attempt to imitate any animal or object, but rather try to show how inner feelings and moods may be expressed through dance movement. Since this is so closely allied to dramatic play it is described in detail in that chapter.

## Improving Rhythmic Skills

One obvious purpose of creative dance experience is to help children understand and enjoy music better. They are given experience in playing simple rhythm instruments and gradually learn about such musical elements as time, accent, meter, phrasing, rhythmic pattern, intensity, and tempo. By experiencing fine classical or modern music (both through listening and moving to it) they are endowed with rich emotional experiences and aesthetic sensations that will undoubtedly improve their attitude toward music in adult life.

At the outset they may listen to musical selections which the teacher or play leader feels will be interesting or attractive to them (or which they have chosen themselves). Gradually they can begin to dance to such accompaniment. This may be done in a completely free, unguided fashion. However, in the case of music which is not "story" music and has no recognizable content, it may be desirable for the teacher or play leader to help them recognize what the basic themes are, what instruments are playing at certain times, what the sections are like, where the music changes, and, possibly, what sorts of actions might logically fit. With this background they are not as likely to feel lost in dancing to such abstract accompaniment.

Natalie Cole, in her text *The Arts in the Classroom,*[35] describes how she works with children in the intermediate grades in such a setting. Occasionally she gives suggestions to the group or develops concepts of body movements. Slowly she helps them develop a sequence of action suited to a particular selection; she may help them divide into groups which are active during different parts of the music. At all times she is praising, encouraging, urging children into participation, and creating an atmosphere where children feel free to let down bars of resistance and really "feel" the music and express the beauty that surges within them.

A somewhat different phase of this topic is that of developing specific rhythmic skills and understanding through the use of certain devices, games, stunts, and exercises. Since these often are carried on with little body activity and since they are so closely linked with music, they are described in the chapter on recreational music.

## Improving Movement Skills

It has already been pointed out that when children reach the intermediate and later elementary grades, they may wish to have more knowledge and greater technical facility of movement than in the early grades. This change is similar to the child's lessened interest in make-believe and play based on fantasy and his increased concern with realistic themes based on the life about him. It means that he is less satisfied by aimless, naïve, and haphazard physical expression and wishes to know what and how he is doing. Also, because he has more opportunity to watch skilled adult dancers in the concert or popular field and to be impressed by their performing talents, he is likely to be favorably motivated toward improving his movement skills.

With this in mind the adult leader or teacher may begin to direct children in exercises or drills that are somewhat similar to modern dance or ballet warm-ups. These represent swings, falls, leaps, turns, stretches, strengthening exercises, and floor patterns that are designed to show children exactly *how* to use their bodies most effectively. Such exercises are learned carefully and slowly, with the function of each part of the body clearly presented and thoroughly practiced and with the timing of the entire movement definitely established. They result in reinforced rhythm, grace, balance, security, strength, and poise, and in giving children a broad vocabulary of movement to use in creative work.

While some of this material may come from improvisations of the children themselves (based on folk and other dance experiences), most of it must come from the adult leader or teacher. This suggests the need for the teacher herself to have some technical training in dance if she wishes to extend her dance classes or groups to this point.

## Group Compositions

At a fairly early point in their total dance experience children may begin to develop simple group compositions. These are desirable because they bring about social interaction and because there are so many more possibilities for interesting dance expression when numbers of participants are involved. It is somewhat like comparing the construction potentialities of one building block to ten blocks. The process of developing group compositions depends on several essential factors:

1. The previous experience of the children in rhythms, mimetic play, and movement skills and the kinds of expressive opportunities they have had in the fields of the language and graphic arts

2. Their ability to function cooperatively in group projects demanding give-and-take

3. The selection of suitable themes and devices for developing compositions

Such themes may be varied; they may be poems, songs and stories, experiences of children, folk materials, abstract forms (such as geometrical forms), relationships, social studies content, or musical selections.

In the primary grades children may first make up individual compositions to familiar nursery rhymes, songs, simple little stories about people or things in their lives, or elements of nature. These may be expanded to include several children playing different roles. Gradually such plots may be made more complex. Here are some samples:

1. "An airplane takes off from a landing field. It flies along, runs into a terrible thunder storm. It battles the storm for a while and finally returns safely to the field."

2. "A giant tree stands in the forest. Woodcutters come along with axes and saws. They cut it down and haul it off to make lumber for homes."

3. "A spider lurks, hidden in a web. A pretty butterfly dances around, coming closer and closer to the web. Finally the spider springs out and catches it in the web. The ending may be happy or sad—depending on how the children feel that day (they make the decision)."

4. "Indians are suffering from famine. They dance around a campfire, praying for food. A messenger runs up, telling of a nearby buffalo herd. They ride out, attack the herd, and get food enough to save the tribe."

*Songs and Poems.* Children may select familiar songs of a somewhat more advanced level to work out dance compositions to. "Working on the Railroad" is a good possibility. To this, they may choose to develop literal action, such as swinging a pick and shovel, pretending to mop their perspiring foreheads, playing a banjo, or being a train shuffling along. They may also choose to do more abstract movements or actions taken from folk dances, in various formations. There may be a division of roles, with some children being the railroad workers and others being a train or even trees along the road-bed. The possibilities are endless.

There are many ways of handling accompaniment. Children may dance while a record is playing. They may sing while they dance. Some children may be on the side lines playing rhythm instruments and/or singing while the others dance. The teacher may accompany them on the piano. Instead of singing all the words, they may chant some of them in choral-speaking fashion. Also, in terms of setting, properties, sound effects, and accessories to the dance such as costumes, they can use their ingenuity to make use of whatever objects are available.

Here is a poem which can be used to develop group compositions with children in the first two or three grades.[36] They might say it over slowly, listening to it and visualizing the kinds of action that might be suitable.

HOW THE ANIMALS MOVE

The lion, he has paws with claws; the horse he walks on hooves.
The worm, he lives right on the ground and wiggles when he moves.
The seal, he moves with swimming feet,

The moth has wings like a sail;
The fly, he clings; the bird, he wings;
The monkey swings by his tail. . . .

Usually it is best to use verses or songs that have clear-cut rhythmic patterns and repeated action choruses that are long enough to permit children to continue moving to them for a period of time. "How the Animals Move" offers one image after another, in fairly quick succession. Children might choose to say each line, pause after it, and then have members of the group, either individually or together, show the action that has occurred to them. Other youngsters might serve as a rhythm orchestra, beating out accompaniment with instruments that seem suitable (and picking up the rhythm from the movement of the dancers). They might use hollow wood blocks for the galloping sound of the horse or a lively tambourine for the swinging monkey. They might have one child do each of the animals suggested and then have all come in together on "boys and girls." Or the entire group might do the action together from the very beginning. If a large class or group is divided into several smaller groups to work on this poem, each one will almost certainly come up with a different and interesting treatment of it.

In the song category, many ballads are particularly useful because their narratives offer different characters and actions which children enjoy dancing out. One example is the old English ballad, "Froggie Went A-courting": [37]

Froggie went a'courting, he did ride, Oh Yes, Uh Hum.
Froggie went a'courting, he did ride,
Sword and pistol by his side, Oh Yes, Uh Hum.

The tale continues: Froggie rides up to Miss Mousie's door and knocks on it. He courts Miss Mousie, and gets permission to marry her from fat Uncle Rat. The three of them search for the wedding supper, and find it under an old oak tree. There they eat and dance to the fiddle music of the nimble cricket, together with other guests, the little flea and the bumblebee—until the uninvited villain, Old Tom Cat, scares them all away. It makes a lively story and children may develop many ways of dancing, singing, and accompanying it with excitement, humor, and suspense.

There are many other possibilities for group compositions. The subject matter need not be trivial or light. The author has seen a very moving dance interpretation of "America, the Beautiful," made up by twelve-year-old boys and girls in Atlanta, Georgia.

He once witnessed a dance composition, made up by children who lived in a cooperative home development, that was based on their daily lives and was presented as the culminating event of a summer's end neighborhood carnival. It was directed by an adult leader, a man who, while not a dancer himself, was a painter and extremely sensitive and receptive to the ideas of the children. He used a drum to give rhythmic accompaniment and spoke the lines that he and the children had worked out together. The story was fascinating in its scope. It embraced the entire universe—the night, moon, stars, sun gradually rising, tides of the ocean beating against the shore. All this was intermittently blended with the life of the family— getting up in the morning, dressing and eating, father rushing to catch a bus to get off to work, children going to school, mother working hard at home, father in the office, children playing sports in the afternoon. It was the entire cycle of life as these eight-to-thirteen-year-olds knew it and it represent an ingenious and appealing child's eye view, welded together by an adult leader who had the good sense not to try to shape or modify it too much. It was the high point of the carnival and justified the time and effort the children had spent on preparing it.

Many themes may be dealt with which, at first glance, might appear to be completely unchildlike. C. Madeleine Dixon, in her interesting book, *The Power of Dance*,[38] describes how different groups of children in private schools in the late 1930's worked out dance compositions on such diverse and adult themes as "The Fields—Planting, Energy, Sun," "Exile—Lullaby, Wandering," "Revolt Against Dictators," and such subjects as racial groups, world religions, and war and peace. These children took the subject matter of the dances extremely seriously (it undoubtedly was a reflection and outgrowth of many other school experiences) and in many cases achieved exceptionally beautiful dance expressions.

In all such experiences children become aware of certain elements of art which tend to make the product a good or a bad one. While the leader should not try to impose rigid rules, there are certain basic principles of art form:

*Unity.* Any art form must have a unified structure in which the design and the content are consistent with each other and the result of the same basic motivating impulse.

*Variety.* There should be a variety of different forms (lines, masses, colors, etc.), which should contrast with each other to achieve interest and yet be in essential harmony, proportion, and balance with each other (except where distortion or disharmony suits the composer's purpose).

*Transition.* Movements or sections of any composition should flow smoothly from one to the next and should be arranged in a purposeful, logical sequence.

*Climax.* Any composition extending through time (as opposed to a painting or piece of sculpture which is fixed in time) should build up to an ending which brings about a feeling of completion and achievement.

Elizabeth Hayes has written of these principles for high school and college dance classes; [39] however, some of her comments apply to children of elementary school age who are attempting ambitious projects in dance composition like the last ones described:

> The primary function of all the aesthetic principles of form—the need for unity, for variety, for repetition, for contrast, for transition, for appropriate sequence, for climax, for pleasing proportion, for balance, and for harmony—is to reveal and illumine the *creative idea,* aiding in its externalization.

A final important aspect of dance composition is that it gives children a chance to get together after a composition has been developed and danced to discuss it fully. Did it say what they wanted it to say? Was it fun to be in? What was best about it? What parts did not succeed well? Did the accompaniment contribute to it? Did they make use of the ideas and talents of all the children? Was the composition something that they might possibly want to go further with and perform before others?

Such evaluative sessions, carried on by the children with the teacher's help when necessary, make an important contribution to their growing social maturity and help each individual child develop desirable attitudes and habits of thoughtful analysis.

## Boys in Creative Dance

Throughout this chapter, which has taken for granted the participation of both sexes, some readers may have been skeptical about the feelings of boys toward any activity as expressive and creative as dance. It must be understood that, in terms of potential interest and skill, boys and men are fully comparable to girls and women. There have been many great male dancers and choreographers, such as Nijinsky, Ted Shawn, Michel Fokine, Leonid Massine, Jose Limon, and others. In many primitive cultures and in the early history of ballet in Europe, men have been the featured, and sometimes the only, dancers. In the dance of the musical stage and moving pictures, there have been many outstanding male performers, such as Gene Kelly, Fred Astaire, and Bill Robinson.

Every young boy can get a great deal of pleasure out of dance—if he is certain that he is not going to be considered a "sissy" because of it. Therefore it is necessary for an atmosphere to be established that makes it completely accepted for a boy to dance. Ideally this can be done with the help of men teachers and recreation leaders (particularly athletic coaches) and by making sure that the sort of dance experience offered to boys is suitable for them in terms of vigorous, exciting physical activity and thoroughly masculine and virile themes for creative expression. Photographs in a number of the books that are listed in the bibliography (Dixon, Andrews, and Cole) show how enthusiastically boys may take part in creative dance. Recent articles in the *Journal of the American Association for Health, Physical Education and Recreation* [40] describe how modern dance has successfully been carried on with boys of high school and college age.

Provided that it is intelligently approached and capably led, creative dance is one of the most rewarding play experiences a child may take part in at any age, or of either sex.

## Summary

This chapter describes various approaches to the field of creative dance, with regard to objectives, materials, and leadership techniques. The development of rhythmic and movement skills are outlined, including simple rhythmic play, pantomimic action, the integration of language materials and social studies units, and group compositions. The following chapters, on music and dramatics, contain additional materials useful in this area.

# CHAPTER 9

# FUN WITH MUSIC

Although this chapter is chiefly concerned with music as a play experience, many of the ideas and activities suggested in it might readily apply to the school music class. In both settings music is seen as a means of making the child's life fuller and happier. In each, the goal is to give youngsters favorable attitudes about music and, within limits, to cultivate certain skills and understandings.

Particularly in play sessions the leader should not place emphasis on teaching specific performing skills or on having children memorize a broad repertoire of musical selections. Activity should be geared to meet the needs and interests of all the children, rather than those few who may have outstanding musical gifts. Such youngsters may certainly be encouraged to develop themselves further, but this is not the chief purpose of musical play.

There are many reasons why parents and teachers agree that musical expression is important for children. It serves as a valuable creative outlet; it is an important asset in their developing social and cultural personalities; and it is an enjoyable recreational pastime that should remain with them throughout life. It should be cautioned, however, that when music is viewed chiefly as a means of gaining social popularity and the applause of others, its motive is perverted and it loses its greatest value.

## Music in Children's Lives

How may musical growth and understanding best be achieved in the everyday lives of children?

A few decades ago the ready answer would have been, "Through regular music lessons at the piano or violin!" Today this answer is not generally accepted. For many young children any approach to music that

142

involves learning scales, reading notes, or fingering an instrument tends to discourage enthusiasm and interest long before the ability to achieve real musical expression is gained. Or if children do persevere or are forced to continue with their lessons, as Satis Coleman comments, they often settle down to cold, mechanical playing.

Instead of a lesson approach, music should be a part of the child's everyday life. Beatrice Landeck writes: [41]

> Music comes from within; it cannot be applied externally. . . . Appreciation of music develops gradually through the years when parents (or teachers) and children are playing, laughing and singing together. Your attitude about music is far more important than any training you have had or may acquire.

Just what *is* the adult's role in this process? Must a parent be highly skilled, either in playing ability or in knowledge of music theory or history, to guide children in musical experiences? On the contrary, such a highly developed background may actually be a hindrance, since serious music, approached on an adult level, may often be boring, confusing, or unpleasant for young children. Instead, it must be closely related to their range of appreciation and understanding, interests, and attention span if it is to appeal to them.

At no time should music be viewed as primarily intellectual experience. Instead, it should be seen as a fascinating and enjoyable form of recreation. As much as possible it should become a common element in the lives of all those in the family and community, both old and young.

How is this to be done?

Actual participation in singing and rhythmic play is, of course, essential. However, there are many other ways in which children can be helped to become aware of, and sensitive to, the great world of existing music. Operas, classical selections (concertos, symphonies, and choral works), and musical plays may all be experienced to some degree, particularly if a wise selection is made of works that are most likely to appeal to children. This growing acquaintanceship may be furthered both in the home and in the community.

*Family Music.* Parents and children may play and sing and enjoy music together on many occasions. Radio and television schedules may be watched for and clipped from newspapers so that when a special event is to occur, it is made a highlight of the evening or weekend for everyone to enjoy.

The family phonograph should be used regularly; a special time may be set aside for music enjoyment. Children may have a special record corner for their own records; in this corner they may also keep a variety of simple rhythm instruments to play with.

From time to time parents and children may go on special music trips or visits to recitals, concerts, and operettas. If such events are not readily available, parents may join together to stimulate community music activities.

*Community Music.* Through Parent-Teacher Associations, church groups, civic associations, or recreation commissions, parents may make a point of sponsoring or stimulating different types of musical programs on a neighborhood or community-wide basis. These may include local gatherings with folk singers, single performers, or instrumentalists, or record concerts. If a well-known performer or teacher of music lives in a community, he may be happy to offer his services occasionally. If there is a nearby school of music or college music department, their students or staff may be available to give programs.

Community recreation centers are likely to offer recitals by choral or instrumental groups from time to time; many towns offer regular series of operettas or concerts by resident or touring companies. Others have summer music centers for children or band concerts sponsored by the local musician's union. All of these may be used to promote community-wide music interest, which results in parents and children taking genuine pleasure in participating on a variety of levels with good, vital music.

## Responding to Music

Many adults do not enjoy music because they feel they do not know "what to listen for." "I don't understand it at all," is a common complaint. Childhood is the time when sound attitudes of music appreciation may best be implanted.

Howard Murphy suggests that there are three chief kinds of responses that human beings have to music: the sensuous, the intellectual, and the spiritual or ethical.[42]

Briefly stated, these are:

*Sensuous.* This is the basic appeal of organized tone, the pleasure derived from the beauty of musical sound that is produced by a voice, instrument, or their combination; it has no special meaning or message.

*Intellectual.* This represents an interest in the organization of music. When one recognizes or analyzes a melody, device of orchestration, musical form, or arrangement of themes, this may be termed an intellectual response.

*Spiritual.* This is the response to music which "elevates" us, or "does us good." Such music, as Murphy puts it, "soars above the material world" and brings us spiritual exaltation.

In listening to music one may experience any or all of these responses.

Certainly it would be pointless to try to have children understand these ways of responding to music in a theoretical way. However, they may be helped to understand the possibilities of listening to music and enjoying it and often to verbalize their feelings about it. Such encouragement will stimulate their sensitivity to the quality of sounds, their awareness of music organization, and their emotional reactions to fine selections. They should be helped to understand, as many adults do not, that some types of music have absolutely no element of literal or "story" meaning and that some others do. They need to be reassured that they need not necessarily look for and find specific meaning in music and that they are entitled to have their own individual reactions to any piece of music.

## What about Music Appreciation?

Traditionally many school music programs have emphasized learning many facts about composers, performers, and famous musical selections. Such concerns do not necessarily result in a child's growing love for music or understanding of it. As Sigmund Spaeth has written: [43]

> . . . I have almost completely disregarded biographical details, believing that the lives of composers become interesting only after their music is a vital reality. . . . It is my firm conviction that a piece of music can be enjoyed regardless of the composer who wrote it, and I believe that the best mental state for a first hearing of any piece of absolute music is one that is empty of all preconceived notions and prejudices.

While this is essentially a sound viewpoint, it is also true that children may also take a deep interest in the background of musical works or outstanding composers or performers—just as they might in famous athletes, scientists, or entertainers in other areas. How may this interest be tactfully cultivated to round out the child's cultural background and enrich his musical understandings? One textbook that is used in schools and that might also be welcome in homes, for children who are old enough to read and appreciate it, is *Music for Young Listeners* by Lillian Baldwin.[44] This book tells about such composers as Handel, Schubert, Mozart, Ravel, and others, and correlates discussion of their works with suggested records.

Another way of encouraging such interest among older children who have already gained some knowledge of the world of music is to play quiz and other games based on musical names, works, and events. Ewen and Slonimsky have published a useful collection of these.[45]

In this broad area of music appreciation, it is important to avoid the attitude that many adults hold, that music is something that someone else does for you. With the wealth of highly professional musical entertainment that is readily available and with the degree of technical perfection that this music has reached, often parents and adult leaders may feel that "home-grown music" is weak and inexpert. Landeck points out that children, on the other hand, want the experience of making music themselves. This sort of expression, close to their own lives and temperaments, is the best and most personal kind of musical experience they can have.

## Singing

The most direct, natural, and enjoyable form of musical play for children is singing. The impulse to sing begins early and lasts for life if it is not inhibited or misdirected by well-meaning adults.

What is a sound approach to the guidance and stimulation of childhood singing? The answer may be dramatized by contrasting two television shows:

On a Sunday morning program Charity Bailey, an experienced music teacher, worked with a group of children who ranged in age through the elementary grades. She played the piano and sometimes the guitar or auto-harp as the children enjoyed a variety of songs, drawn chiefly from the folk category. Most of the songs were already familiar to them; others were quickly and easily taught. Often Miss Bailey told the children something about the background of a song when she felt it would enrich the experience for them. Sometimes the children danced freely to songs; at other times they did traditional versions of singing games and folk dances. Regularly they accompanied a melody or two with rhythm instruments. At all times the teacher gently encouraged the children, accepting mistakes in good humor, never trying for perfection, but always emphasizing the musical values of each song. Watching the faces of the children, one saw intense interest and pleasure—but never strain, although they were certainly aware that a television camera was focused on them.

This program was immediately followed by an hour-long show which had been featured on radio and television for many years. Here children danced and sang like little adults. They did complicated tap dance and ballet arrangements and sang adult blues and Tin Pan Alley songs, like miniature editions of Frankie Laine or Johnny Ray—with all the characteristics of quavering voice and fluttering hands. This had nothing to do with singing for fun; instead, these youngsters were working toward big-time careers in the professional entertainment world.

This second program, while it had superficial appeal and allure and probably was considered by the sponsor and network more commercially effective for a mass television audience, was certainly not a good example of children singing and dancing for their own amusement and musical growth. Yet it demonstrated vividly how great numbers of parents are influenced in their thinking about the musical education of their children.

The starting point for outlining a sensible approach to guiding childhood singing might be in terms of the songs that are presented.

*Selecting Songs.* There are many useful kinds of song materials. They may be drawn from the categories of patriotic music, religious hymns and spirituals, camp songs, old popular favorites, songs of other lands, and others. The important criteria are that the music be strongly melodic, easy to sing but still interesting, have strong rhythmic flow, that the themes and word content be suitable for children, and that it be pitched suitably for them.

Many music teachers agree, however, that the best single category of music for children is the folk song—the tune of anonymous origin that has been handed down from generation to generation—"the kind that travels and the stuff that sticks."

Why? Beatrice Landeck comments [46] that:

Good songs are a human chronicle revealing the innermost sentiments of those who spontaneously made them; American folk songs are for us the most meaningful songs. The mere fact that most of them have lasted for many generations means that their themes are real and important, the ideas they express gripping and entertaining. . . .

In folk songs one finds colorful language, vivid imagery, humor, and warmth. Their themes range from cowboy, sailing, and mining songs to tender ballads of love or tragedy; from gay nonsense ditties and tall tales to history come alive through music.

In a good folk song the words and melody are often so well paired that they support and strengthen each other and need not be separated for teaching. Many folk songs have repeated choruses which children may learn and sing along with immediately. In some songs the rhyming pattern is so apparent that children can guess and sing the final word without being told it in advance. This may even be played as a game:

If you love me, Liza Jane, put your hand in mine,
You won't lack for no corn bread, as long as the sun do ————.

"Shine" is the word, and any child will supply it for you without having heard the song before.

This example suggests a problem connected with some folk songs. Often they are so informal or regional in origin that they make use of mis-pronunciations, poor grammar, and slang words. A child may wonder why it's all right to sing "g'wine" or "ain't" when it isn't considered proper to talk that way. Since folk songs are traditionally changed as they pass from person to person, an adult should feel free to change the words of a song if they bother him in this way—although he should always try to retain the original flavor of a song whenever possible. And if this involves drop-ping a few final "g's" or slurring some other words, no real harm is done.

Another concern that some parents and teachers have about folk songs is that they occasionally deal with such ideas as death and dying, unrequited love, or physical violence. Ruth Crawford Seeger, author of *American Folk Songs for Children*,[47] asks whether it is ever possible to shield children from the knowledge of such things happening. Or, realizing that there may be pain and brutality and sadness in life, may not a child be helped to better accept such things and fear them less?

If a song is too gruesome, like the traditional singing game "The Roman Soldiers" (in which youngsters engage in a mock battle and grad-ually lose limb after limb), no parent or teacher may wish to use it. On the other hand, the ballad, "Old Blue" tells in a beautiful way about the death of a beloved hound dog:

When old Blue died he died so hard
He shook the ground in my back yard.
Old Blue died, I laid him in the shade
I dug his grave with a silver spade.

Might not such a song reduce the child's fear of death and give him a sense of life continuing?

## SINGING FOR YOUNGER CHILDREN

When singing with children in small preschool groups and even through the primary grades, leaders should be extremely informal and natural and do a minimum of teaching as such. Seeger suggests that the emphasis should always be on the song itself, rather than on the quality of its performance. Thus the desired comment is, "That sure is a good song," rather than, "You sang it well." Folk songs should be presented without affectation, self-consciousness, or attempts to get dramatic effects.

The accompaniment of such songs need not be elaborate or expert. Simple chording on the guitar or autoharp should be more than enough to give the basic rhythm and pitch of most folk tunes; many others may be done with hand-clapping, finger-snapping, or no accompaniment at all.

Being able to play a piano is a great advantage, in terms of being able to present melody strongly. However, with little children, it may make the situation too formal and put the leader at too great a distance. Particularly if the piano is played too strongly, there may be a tendency for them just to sit and listen, rather than sing freely themselves. When this happens—indeed, always, with very young children—the leader should try sitting with them so that they are all facing in small groups.

The leader should not always expect all the children to respond in a strong, active way. Often children who do not appear to be singing or even to be paying attention are actually interested and taking in everything that goes on. One child who attended a folk song concert by a well-known recording artist showed boredom, squirmed continually, and finally was taken out of the hall. The parents decided that it had been a poor idea, and that she was too young for this type of experience. However, for several weeks afterward she sang snatches of songs she had heard at the recital, referred to it constantly, and apparently recalled it with great pleasure.

Group singing with small children is never neat and well-organized; often songs are stop-and-go and punctuated by comments, irrelevant questions, and other kinds of disruptive behavior. If the leader can simply be quite relaxed about the whole thing and feel free to approach the session in a leisurely, easygoing way, half the battle will be won.

It is wise to repeat new songs again and again; let children get used to them easily and gradually. As the melody and words become familiar, children will often improvise on them with changes and ideas that grow out of their environment. They are likely, with a song like "Cindy," or, indeed, with any familiar melody, to suggest many verses about working, cleaning up, painting, friends, animals, and family. One group of inter-mediate-grade children made up the following parody of the then-popular "Sixteen Tons":

> You take sixteen kids and what do you get?
> Another day older and deeper in debt.
> St. Peter, don't you call me, 'cause I can't go,
> I owe my soul to the Principal.

In any singing session with young children they are likely to suggest many such changes, often of a nonsense nature. Singing may become a game with them, particularly when the leader introduces tall-tale songs, "answer-back" songs, "make-up" songs and note and word-guessing. It is a good idea to do many lively action songs but also to introduce a number of quiet songs which place greater stress on the quality of the sound or on real musical feeling. The leader need never be in a hurry to race from one song to another; it is paradoxical of youngsters that, while they may have short attention spans while learning new material, they often like to stick with the same song for quite a period of time, savoring its flavor and turning it over and over.

Informal song leadership of this kind may also be carried on with small, face-to-face groups of older children. Songs may be casually selected at the suggestion of participants; different youngsters may be called on to sing solo parts, and to improvise verses and parodies. There may be easy-going banter between songs, and the leader need not take a major amount of responsibility in directing the singing if the children themselves know enough good songs to keep the activity going in a lively way.

However, when singing is being carried on with a large group of older children such as a school assembly program or interclub meeting, the situation demands stronger leadership and a greater degree of control and planning.

SINGING WITH LARGER GROUPS

When working with a group of over twenty or thirty, it is necessary that the leader take into account the following factors: (1) means of teaching new songs; (2) accompaniment; (3) getting full participation; and (4) **conducting techniques.**

*Means of Teaching New Songs.* With large groups it becomes somewhat more difficult to teach the words and melodies of new songs than with informal groups. Therefore the leader should include fewer of these on his preplanned program (which should be structured carefully in advance, with some allowance for changes), and should pick those which can be easily learned by the group. A good type of song is one which has a repeated chorus that can be learned at once and sung successfully by all the participants. A more difficult type is a ballad or other song which has many unfamiliar verses.

Sometimes in presenting new material a leader may distribute mimeographed song sheets or use slides to project the words on a screen. However, these detract from the attention given to the leader and should be used with caution.

Whenever a song requires considerable teaching, it should be sandwiched into the program between others that are thoroughly familiar. Familiar songs should also be used at the beginning of a song session to "get off on the right foot," and, in most cases, at the end, so that the final impression will be one of successful accomplishment.

*Accompaniment.* In small groups the leader may use no instrument at all or a simple rhythmic one, such as a ukulele or guitar, which does not provide much melody. However, the problem of getting the melody across to a larger group and of keeping them all together often makes it desirable to have the accompaniment of a piano or accordion. It is possible for a leader to use such an instrument and direct singing at the same time, but in order to free him to work more effectively with the group, he will find it most convenient to have another person acting as accompanist.

The accompanist should not merely follow the melody but should act as a second leader. He should provide a strong rhythmic background with a degree of volume that is in good balance with the singing of the group. The accompanist should be able to watch the leader at all times so that he can follow his directions and signals when a song is begun or ended or when special effects are needed.

A good accompanist is flexible; when the singers are quite familiar with the selection being done, he should feel free to harmonize and play countermelodies and rhythms. When it is new to most of them, he should play the correct melody clearly and distinctly so they will not be confused about it.

The leader need not feel that he must use the accompanist for all songs; often he may find that the group responds best to a soft, reverent type of song if they are asked to sing it quietly and gently with no accompaniment.

*Getting Full Participation.* This, of course, is a major challenge in leading any play activity, but it is particularly important when singing with a large group since a few youngsters who are not interested may ruin the singing for the rest—simply by talking noisily or deliberately singing in a raucous, disruptive way.

How can the leader interest and involve all the participants? The simplest reply is to pick the most enjoyable songs and to lead them with enthusiasm so that the musical effect brings pleasure to all the youngsters present. It helps for him to make a good initial impression and it is essential that he focus his attention and directions on *all* the participants, rather than on just the few who are directly in front of him. He may do this by moving about, by shifting his gaze and gestures from one section to another, and by doing rounds or other part songs in which all the singers are involved in special ways.

Children may also become rebellious if the leader is too negatively critical or if instruction of a particular song takes too long. Thus he should always keep positive and buoyant and, if he must correct aspects of the singing, do it in a humorous, impersonal way. In teaching words or melody he should attempt to do it with fairly long phrases which are learned and then linked together, rather than by chopping it up into many stop-and-go phrases. If any song proves too difficult or long to do successfully all at once, the leader may decide to drop it for a time, and return to it at a later session.

*Conducting Techniques.* While it is not necessary for the recreational song leader to have all the formal skills of the professional choral director, it is helpful for him to be able to use certain gestures in directing singing. Augustus Zanzig [48] suggests certain types of movements which may be used to help make singing unified and strong:

1. To welcome the participants or to begin singing, hands should be raised or held out to the sides and forward. When the group is ready, the leader makes a clear-cut downward movement to start the song.

2. To encourage singers to hold a long note, the left hand may be held up while the right hand continues to mark the beats. If the note to be held is very full and rich, the left fist may be strongly clenched.

3. The leader should make his gestures small for soft singing and large for loud singing. To make the singing quieter and gentler, he may use his left hand in a gentle downward motion, with palm turned down. To

encourage greater volume, the left hand may be used with a lively upward gesture.

4. In beating time there are certain specific movements to indicate various meters (Diagrams 30-A, 30-B, 30-C). The amateur song leader may not learn to do these movements with professional polish, but he should

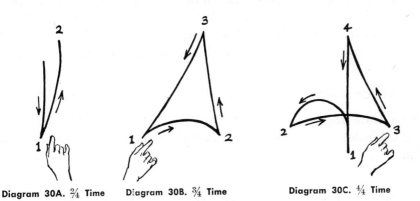

Diagram 30A. 2/4 Time    Diagram 30B. 3/4 Time      Diagram 30C. 4/4 Time

attempt to convey at least the pulse and accent of the song to the participants through hand and arm gestures. In addition, by using his entire body flexibly and expressively, he can heighten the particular quality of each song, emphasize its various climaxes and changes, and convey, through his facial expression, the mood.

5. To end a particular song or section of a song, the leader should use a recognizable gesture such as a rounded hand-motion in the air.

Other points stressed by Zanzig are that the leader should know many useful songs and should not hesitate to vary the mood and quality of singing during a single session. Action songs may often be used, as well as songs that go from soft to loud and vice versa. Some songs should be done in unison; others should have solo parts. Often it helps to divide a group into sections and have them listen to part of the song to help them become more aware of its musical quality.

The following section includes examples of various types of songs that are useful for recreational singing with children. Some are "dialogue" or "answer-back" songs. Others are "make-up" songs. Some involve actions; others have different parts for different groups of singers. Some are soft and gentle; others lively and loud. Most of them tend to be in the novelty category. The reader should not conclude from this that a song must be "tricked-up" in order to be effective. There are many wonderful songs that have nothing novel about them whatever but simply provide joyous singing, and these should prove a major part of any song session. They are, however, familiar to most readers already, and therefore the emphasis in this chapter is placed on those songs which are less likely to be well-known.

The musical arrangements, as prepared by Deborah Hunt Jennings, contain melody lines (experienced musicians may improvise their own accompaniments) and letter chords for those who play such instruments as the guitar, ukulele, or autoharp. Each tune has been placed in a key that will be comfortable both for the adult leader and the children to sing in.

### COWBOY SONGS

#### Roll on, Little Dogies

Here is a quiet cowboy song with a chorus so simple that it almost sings itself.

CHORUS:  Roll on, roll on, roll on, little dogies,
         Roll on, roll on.
         Roll on, roll on, roll on, little dogies, roll on.

1.  Last night as I lay on my pillow,
        And looked at the stars in the sky,
    I wondered if ever a cowboy,
        Would reach that sweet bye-and-bye.

## Chisholm Trail

This lively ballad has innumerable verses telling of the hard life of the cowboy on the famed Chisholm cattle trail.

1. Oh, come along boys, and listen to my tale,
    I'll tell you of my troubles, on the old Chisholm trail,

CHORUS:   Come–a–ti–yi–yippy–yippy–yip–yippy–yay,
          Come–a–ti–yi–yippy–yippy–yay.

2. It's up in the morning, afore daylight,
    By the time I sleep, the moon shines bright.
3. It's bacon and beans most every day,
    I'd as soon be eating prairie hay.
4. It's cloudy in the West, and looking like rain,
    And my durned old slicker's in the wagon again.
5. I went to the boss, for to draw my roll,
    He had me figured out nine dollars in the hole.
6. With my feet in the stirrups and my hat in the sky,
    I'll quit punching cows in the sweet bye-and-bye.

**SEA CHANTEY**

### Sacramento

This song tells the story of the Gold Rush of '49, when fast California clipper ships took the water route around Cape Horn in a wild race for fortune.

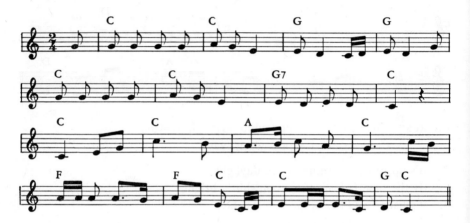

1. [Solo]     A bully ship and a bully crew,
   [Group]    Doo–da, doo–da.
   [Solo]     A bully mate and a captain too,
   [Group]    Doo–da, doo–da–day.
   CHORUS:   Then blow ye winds, hi–oh,
                    For Californy–o!
                    There's plenty of gold, so I've been told,
                    On the banks of the Sacramento!

**ACTION SONG**

## Where Is Thumbkin?

This is a simple action song with finger-play for younger children.

1. Where is thumbkin?        [hands are hidden behind singers back]
   Where is thumbkin?
   Here I am.               [right fist makes appearance, thumb point-
                              ing up]

   Here I am.               [left fist appears, same way]
   How are you today, sir?  [right thumb "nods" rapidly]
   Very well, I thank you.  [left thumb does the same]
   Run away.               [right hand disappears behind back]
   Run away.               [left hand does the same]

## NONSENSE SONGS

### Uncle Reuben

Many folk songs have nonsense syllables which mean little but are fun to sing. A simple example is "Uncle Reuben."

CHORUS:  Uncle Reuben got a coon, done gone, chick–a–chick,
Done gone, chick–a–chick, done gone, chick–a–chick,
Uncle Reuben got a coon, done gone, chick–a–chick,
And left me here behind.

1. If you love me, Liza Jane, put your hand in mine.
You won't lack for no corn bread, as long as the sun do shine.
2. Possum up a 'simmon tree, raccoon on the ground,
Raccoon say, "Mister possum, won't you shake one 'simmon down?"

## Sourwood Mountain

Another folk song with repeated chorus and a somewhat more complicated set of nonsense syllables is "Sourwood Mountain."

1. Chicken crowing on Sourwood mountain,
     Hey–de–ing–dang, diddle–ally–day.
   So many pretty girls I can't count 'em,
     Hey–de–ing–dang, diddle–ally–day.
2. My true love's a blue-eyed daisy, etc.
   If I don't get her I'll go crazy, etc.
3. My true love lives up the river, etc.
   A few more jumps and I'll be with her, etc.
4. My true love lives up the hollow, etc.
   She won't come and I won't follow, etc.
5. Big dog'll bark and little dog'll bite you, etc.
   Big girl'll court and little one'll slight you, etc.

### REPEATED LINES

## Go Tell Aunt Rhody

In this song the first line of each verse is repeated twice more, which makes it easy to sing on the spur of the moment. The mood is a plaintive one.

1.  Go tell Aunt Rhody,   go tell aunt Rhody,
    Go tell Aunt Rhody,   that the old gray goose is dead.
2.  The goslin's are cryin',   the goslin's are cryin',
    The goslin's are cryin',   because their mammy's dead.
3.  The old gander's mournin',   the old gander's mournin',
    The old gander's mournin',   because his wife is dead.
4.  She died in the millpond,   died in the millpond,
    She died in the millpond,   standin' on her head.

## SONGS OF EXAGGERATION

### The Gray Goose

Another song about a goose—but, unlike Aunt Rhody's gray goose, this
one refused to die.

1. Last Sunday morning, Lord, Lord, Lord,
   Last Sunday morning, Lord, Lord, Lord.
2. Oh, my daddy went a-hunting, Lord, Lord, Lord,
   My daddy went a-hunting, Lord, Lord, Lord.
3. And he took along his shotgun, Lord, Lord, Lord,
   He took along his shotgun, Lord, Lord, Lord.
4. And along came a gray goose, etc.
5. The gun went off a-booloo, etc.
6. He was six weeks a-falling, etc.
7. Then they had a feather-picking, etc.
8. Your wife and my wife, etc.
9. And he was nine months a-cooking, etc.
10. Then they put him on the table, etc.
11. But the knife couldn't cut him, etc.
12. And the fork couldn't stick him, etc.
13. So they took him to the hogpen, etc.
14. But the hogs couldn't eat him, etc.
15. And the last time I see'd him, etc.
16. He was flying o'er the ocean, etc.
17. With a long string of goslin's, etc.
18. They was all a-going "Quink, quank," etc.

(At end, all shout) "That was some gray goose!"

## Hush, Little Baby

Children enjoy singing this lullaby; although it has no repeated lines or choruses, its rhyming scheme helps them remember the words.

1. Hush, little baby, don't say a word,
   Mama's going to buy you a mocking bird.
2. And if that mocking bird don't sing,
   Mama's going to buy you a diamond ring.
3. And if that diamond ring turn brass,
   Mama's going to buy you a looking glass.
4. And if that looking glass get broke,
   Mama's going to buy you a billy goat.
5. And if that billy goat don't pull,
   Mama's going to buy you a cart and bull.
6. If that cart and bull turn over,
   Mama's going to buy you a dog named Rover.
7. If that dog named Rover don't bark,
   Mama's going to buy you a horse and cart.
8. If that horse and cart fall down,
   You'll be the sweetest little baby in town.

## Froggie Went A-courtin'

This old ballad has many variations. Because of the comical story it tells and the animal characters that play a part in it, it lends itself well to dance dramatization.

1. Froggie went a-courtin', he did ride, Oh yes, Uh-Huh,
   Froggie went a-courtin', he did ride,
   Sword and pistol by his side, Oh yes, Uh-Huh.

2. He rode up to Miss Mousie's door, etc.
   And knocked and knocked 'til his fist got sore, etc.

3. He said, "Miss Mousie, will you marry me?" etc.
   "For I'm in love, as plain as can be," etc.

4. "Oh, I can't give you the answer to that," etc.
   "You'll have to ask my Uncle Rat," etc.

5. Uncle Rat laughed, and chucked his fat sides, etc.
   To think his niece would be a bride, etc.

6. Now, where will the wedding supper be? etc.
   Way up yonder in the old oak tree, etc.

7. And what will the wedding supper be? etc.
   Turnip greens and a black-eyed pea, etc.

8. The first to come was the humble cricket, etc.
   Took out his fiddle and began to pick it, etc.

9. The next to come was the little flea, etc.
   And he began jigging with a bumble bee, etc.

10. The next to come was the old Tom Cat, etc.
    And he got after Uncle Rat, etc.

11. They all ran up on the shelf, etc.
    If you want any more, you must sing it yourself, etc.

## ADD-ON SONGS

### Bought Me a Cat

"Add-on songs," in which children keep adding new phrases to previous verses, are always popular. This one, because of the "animal sounds" (which are unlike the stereotyped "meow" and "quack, quack"), is especially good.

1. Bought me a cat, the cat pleased me,
   Fed my cat under yonder tree.
   Cat went fiddle–i–fee, fiddle–i–fee.
2. Bought me a hen, the hen pleased me,
   Fed my hen under yonder tree.
   Hen went chip–sy chop–sy,
   Cat went fiddle–i–fee, fiddle–i–fee.

3. Bought me a duck, the duck pleased me,
   Fed my duck under yonder tree.
   Duck went slishy sloshy,
   Hen went chipsy, chopsy.
   Cat went fiddle–i–fee, fiddle–i–fee.

Continue song, adding the following animals and sounds:

| | | | | | |
|---|---|---|---|---|---|
| 4. | Goose | qua | 8. | Horse | neigh |
| 5. | Dog | boo | 9. | Baby | mammy, mammy |
| 6. | Sheep | baa | 10. | Woman | honey, honey |
| 7. | Cow | moo | | | |

## The Twelve Days of Christmas

Another old add-on, or cumulative, song is this English Christmas Carol
describing the twelve days between Christmas day and Epiphany.

1. On the first day of Christmas, my true love sent to me,
   A partridge in a pear tree.
2. On the second day of Christmas, my true love sent to me,
   Two turtle doves and a partridge in a pear tree.
3. On the third day of Christmas, my true love sent to me,
   Three French hens, two turtle doves, and a partridge in a pear tree.

(This continues, adding a new gift for each day, in this sequence:)

4.  Fourth day      four calling birds
5.  Fifth day       five golden rings
6.  Sixth day       six geese a-laying
7.  Seventh day     seven swans a-swimming
8.  Eighth day      eight maids a-milking
9.  Ninth day       nine ladies dancing
10. Tenth day       ten lords a-leaping
11. Eleventh day    eleven pipers piping
12. Twelfth day     twelve drummers drumming

### ADD-ON AND ACTION SONGS

#### If You're Happy

Not only does this song, contributed by Lucile Cordova of New Mexico, add-on phrases, but there is an action for each phrase. It is especially suitable for lively community singing.

1. If you're happy and you know it, clap your hands [clap, clap]
   If you're happy and you know it, clap your hands [clap, clap]
   If you're happy and you know it, then your life will surely show it
   If you're happy and you know it, clap your hands [clap, clap]
2. If you're happy and you know it, stamp your feet [stamp, stamp], etc.
   [at end of this verse, stamp, stamp, then clap, clap]

Continue song, adding following actions: bow your head; shut your eyes; turn around; whistle a tune; say "Amen"; wave goodbye.

At end of each verse, *say* and *do* all preceding actions in order.

## Der Goot Konductor

This is a German-American action song sometimes called "Musikanter." It follows a pattern of having the leader sing the first line and the group respond with a similar line. Obviously the dialect is far from pure German and should be taken in fun!

1.  [Leader] Ich bin der goot konductor, komm from Schwabenland.
    [Group] Du bist der goot konductor, komm from Schwabenland.
    [Leader] Ich kann spielen!
    [Group] Du kannst spielen!
    [Leader] Auf der viola!
    [Group] Auf der viola!
    [All together] Vi–o, Vi–o, Vi–o–la, Vi–o, Vi–o, Vi–o–la,
                   Vi–o, Vi–o, Vi–o–la, Vi–o, Vi–o–la!
    [While singing this, all imitate playing of violin.]

[The following verses are like verse one, except that the instruments are different.]

2.  *Trumpet:* T–ra, T–ra, T–ra–ta–ta, etc. [play trumpet]
3.  *Tuba:* Um–pah, Um–pah, Um–pah–pah, etc. [squeeze sides with arms]
4.  *Fife:* Fee, Fee, Fee, etc. [play fife]
5.  *Drum:* Boom, Boom, Boom, etc. [beat bass drum]
6.  *Dudelsack (Bagpipe):* Wah, Wah, Wah, etc. [puff cheeks while playing]

NOTE:  This is an "add-on" song in that, after each instrument is sung and acted out, the previous instruments are sung and acted out in order before doing the next verse. Children will enjoy making up sounds and actions for new instruments.

## Rhythmic Play

There are, of course, important elements of rhythmic play in the preceding chapters and in those to follow. The chief emphasis in the concluding section of this chapter is on the musical or "sound" aspects of rhythmic play. What are some of the goals of this type of activity, and what are some of the experiences in it that children may be helped to enjoy?

First, it may be helpful to define the term "rhythm." One description is: "the measured release and recovery of energy, consisting of repeated units or patterns, taking form in line and design."

Children are aware of many kinds of rhythm in their lives. They *see* rhythm—in the vertical lines of a picket fence, railroad ties disappearing in the distance, or rows of windows on the face of a giant skyscraper. They *hear* rhythm—in the tick-tock of a kitchen clock, footsteps coming down a hallway, or the clicking wheels of a train. They *touch* rhythm—by running their hands along a grill or the gut strings of a tennis racket. They *feel* rhythm within themselves—in their breathing, heartbeat, and in the repeated patterns (sleeping, rising, eating, playing, and working) of their daily lives. They *sense* rhythm in nature—in the vast elemental forces of night and day, the surge of the oceans, clouds racing across a sky, or the slow changing of the seasons. They *play* in rhythm—running, jumping, clapping, or bouncing a ball.

*Encouraging Rhythmic Expression.* Many opportunities for rhythmic play may be given to young children through the use of phonograph records, singing, and playing with simple percussive instruments. In response to musical stimuli, children should be encouraged to move freely and naturally, rather than in a stereotyped or imitative way. They may also experiment with familiar sounds around them, such as doorbells, water glasses, tools, train whistles, dogs barking, or rain on the roof, using these stimuli as the basis for rhythmic play. Such play may be a combination of singing—either nonsense syllables or more recognizable improvisations—and free movement.

## Use of Rhythm Instruments

In a more organized way, children may be encouraged to play simple rhythm instruments in accompaniment to a phonograph record or a leader's piano playing and singing. The songs that are chosen for them to accompany should be familiar at the outset and should have very recognizable, clear-cut melodies; later some may be chosen which are more complex or unusual, but this is not wise at the beginning.

*Playing the Rhythmic Beat.* At first children would practice playing the basic, underlying rhythmic beat, the regular rhythm that does not change. This beat in "Jingle Bells" would be:

*Jin–*gle *bells, jin–*gle *bells, jin–*gle *all* the *way,*
*Oh* what *fun* it *is* to *ride,* in a *one* horse *o–*pen *sleigh.*

*Playing the Melodic Beat.* When children have become familiar with this way of accompanying and have tried it successfully with a number of songs (and perhaps, also practiced moving about the floor to the rhythmic beat), they may then be sensitized to the rhythm of the melodic line. This may be called the word rhythm, since, in a melody that is sung, that is the easiest way to recognize it. Thus they would accompany "Skip to My Lou" in this way:

Skip, skip, skip to my Lou [three times] Dum, dum, dum–de–de–dum,
Skip to my Lou, My dar – ling.      Dum–de–de–dum, dum dum dum.

When children have practiced beating the melody line with a variety of tunes that have very recognizable note combinations, they have become conscious of note values, and this might be presented to them as a distinct idea, with a musical staff and diagrams.

*Variations.* When they have mastered the skill of accompanying either the rhythmic or melodic beat, children may meet new challenges.

1. Within a single song all the children may play the rhythmic accompaniment during the verses and the melodic accompaniment during the choruses.

2. Within a single song those children who have the deeper, more resonant instruments, such as drums, may play the rhythmic beat throughout, while those who have higher-pitched, tinkling instruments, such as triangles or bells, may play the melodic accompaniment.

Throughout these ventures children should learn the characteristics and special features of each of the rhythm instruments—and how to make the best use of them. The various ways of holding a drum, the different points where it may be struck to produce different kinds of sound, the ways in which the striking hand or beater may be used—all these the children might discover with the leader's help. Throughout they should be encouraged to really listen to each instrument, letting the sound die off slowly while they are experimenting with it. Otherwise there is a danger that they may be satisfied just to beat them wildly and without any real quality; this happens too often when they make use of kitchen implements or improvised sound-makers that have no real musical tone.

From such informal beginnings children may progress to more complicated and highly organized musical arrangements, with each instrument, whether it be wood blocks, scrapers, tambourines, etc., being assigned to special sections of music. Children should play a major part in working out such arrangements, and the experience is valuable and interesting for them. However, when it becomes too complex and when the final musical product is stressed, rather than the fun of playing with music, it may lose some recreational value. In addition, at this point the technical skill required may be beyond that of the average play leader or teacher.

## Other Rhythmic Activities

There are many other games or stunts which involve rhythmic exploration.

**Sending Messages.** This activity involves making up or copying short phrases of drumbeats or hand-clapping. It might be played as a follow-the-leader stunt, in which the leader or one of the children beats out a short phrase which the other children must imitate on their instruments. The leader changes the phrase each time, and the others follow his variations in good rhythm. This may be made more complicated by having the children pass a single drum, one to another, to return the message as the leader keeps sending a new message. It might also be played in reverse, with the big drum being passed from child to child and with each new child receiving it inventing a fresh message which the others must answer back.

**Clapping Songs.** At a very early age children may pick familiar songs or nursery rhymes and practice hand-clapping their melodic patterns. As a game, one child might clap the first line of a song he is thinking of while the other youngsters try to guess what he has in mind. Since they are not likely to know a great many songs, it should not be too difficult for one of them to guess the correct tune.

**Clapping Names.** Children may also practice clapping the rhythm of their individual names. Thus a boy might say, "My name is Peter Mariotti.

Pe - ter. Ma - ri - ot - ti." As he says the name a second time, he simultaneously claps its rhythm, giving each syllable the appropriate length and accent. Then the other children might join in at a signal and clap his name.

Elizabeth Waterman suggests a variation of this in which a name is clapped several times, until its rhythm and musical feeling emerge clearly for the participants. Youngsters may feel that a name suggests a certain specific type of action, such as a walk, run, polka, or skip. Or, because of the rising or falling quality of the sounds or other characteristics, children might interpret the name in terms of a floor movement, such as a "run-run-turn around-and drop," or a "skip-and-jump-jump." This sort of improvisation is best attempted when they have had considerable floor movement already, as described in the preceding chapter.

## Learning from Rhythmic Play

As they proceed with these activities, children may become familiar with various elements of music and rhythm which, in turn, more advanced activities may be based upon. Some concepts that may be made clear to them follow:

They may learn that whenever movement takes place, time is consumed for a definite period or duration; force, or energy, is expended; and space, or distance, is covered.

They learn that the *beat* is the measuring unit for time. *Accent* is the emphasis, or stress, which is placed on a beat or part of a beat. *Tempo* is the rate of speed, ranging from very slow to very fast. *Meter* is the result when regular rhythmic accents serve to group single beats into measures. *Phrase* is a sequence of measures which seem to fit together in a unit as part of a melody. *Force* is the relative strength, or intensity, of a rhythmic beat or combination of beats. *Pitch* is the high or low quality of a musical sound. When applied to movement, they might learn these terms: *design* is a pattern or organized combination of movements. *Direction* is the course of movement. *Level* means the plane, or height, in which a body moves.

In making these terms meaningful, children may explore various subjects in rhythmic play.

**Transportation.** Children may experiment by making up the sound rhythms of various kinds of transportation devices: planes, trains, wagons, etc. They may also take each specific concept and apply it to the problem in this way:

*Force.* Through beating rhythms, and then through movement, show the different intensities of a train, raft on a river, bicycle, etc.

*Tempo.* React to airplane, pogo stick, wheelchair.

*Level.* Explore sled, school bus, and roller-coaster.

Animals offer many interesting possibilities in making these ideas meaningful. One device is to use the animals in a barnyard as a way of showing note values. This would be done after children had become quite familiar with the idea of whole notes, half notes, quarter notes, etc., could identify them on a musical staff, and had practiced beating each of the different note values.

**Barnyard Animals.** This might be begun by having children divide into groups, one group for each value, ranging from eighth notes to whole notes. They might practice playing all at once, with the adult leader giving the basic rhythm by playing on a piano. To vitalize the exercise the leader might ask, "How about the animals in the barnyard? If we were to give each of them a note value according to how quickly or slowly they move, what would it be?"

The children would be quick to suggest ideas. "Make the pig a whole note! He's very slow." "Make the horse a quarter note. He's pretty fast." "Eighth notes should be chickens running after grain." "A cow could be the half note. Sometimes she's almost as slow as a big fat pig."

They might practice beating each of the different note values again and then divide into groups, one for each animal to which a value has been assigned. As part of this exercise they could choose instruments which seemed to suit the nature of the particular animal. A heavy drum might be the pig, or sow. A cow bell could be the cow. Wood blocks might suggest the galloping sound of a horse. Maracas, with their rattling, grainlike sound, would be fine for chickens.

Each group might then play its particular rhythm with its special instruments as the leader sets the basic beat. Then other children might join in groups of horses, cows, chickens, etc. As half the children play rhythm instruments, the others, moving in their own groups, might follow the suggested rhythm for each type of barnyard animal. Finally, when they are thoroughly familiar with the action and can pick their own sounds out clearly from the others, they may be told to move only when they hear their instruments playing. Then the adult leader or a child may act as the "farmer." Without ever stopping the basic beat, he signals the instrumental groups to be silent or to play. At times only one or two may be playing, and at times they may all be playing. The "animal" groups move only when their "rhythmic" group is playing. At the outset there may be a great deal of confusion when this is attempted, but gradually children will get the knack of it and will be able to play it successfully.

The same type of device may be used, with the theme of clocks (grandfather clock slow, wrist watch fast, etc.) or with various types of machines setting the pace (printing press, sewing machine, etc.).

## Experimenting with Meters

Children may also practice playing rhythm instruments in various meters, with the adult leader giving them a strong basic beat. With very young participants each meter may be illustrated visually by showing them toys next to each other. (A big stuffed bear and two little dolls might suggest three-quarter time, for example). Children would identify each meter, count it out, and play it with instruments.

Another approach would be to have them draw or paint different meters. Drawings might emerge in a diagrammatic form, with clear-cut, obvious symbols (not musical notes, however) for each beat. They might also be approached in a more general way, in which children would show their feeling about each meter through the use of lines, masses, etc.

In using rhythm instruments children may select only one or two notes of each measure to play with their instruments. Thus the cymbals might come in only on the accented beat, while finger bells might play the offbeat.

The leader will find that, with encouragement and freedom to explore, children are able to evolve many other playlike ways of approaching the various concepts of tempo, pitch, force, etc., in working with rhythm instruments. Whenever possible, he should vitalize the experience for them by relating what they are doing to their interests, the life around them, and various images that will capture their imagination.

## Summary

This chapter presents a basic philosophy and approach toward musical play—both in recreational and classroom settings. Various types of experiences that lead to favorable attitudes about music are described. A number of suggestions are offered for song leadership in groups large and small, with children of various ages, together with songs illustrating various categories of useful materials. Rhythmic techniques are described in the final section of the chapter.

# CHAPTER 10

# INFORMAL
# DRAMATICS

Anyone who has observed or worked with young children over a period of time knows that they love to play-act; make-believe is an instinctive and joyous part of their lives.

Early dramatic play is at first quite spontaneous. The subject matter may range from building activities to playing house, acting out family happenings, visits to the doctor, going on trips to the zoo or beach, or even to playing out favorite stories read in children's books or seen on television.

This sort of play is obviously not a high form of art; instead, it is usually naïve, crude, incomplete—and honest. At no time should the adult attempt to alter its expression, other than to encourage and appreciate. To stimulate play-acting, the parent or adult leader should give children toys or other materials that lend themselves to story improvisation. The child will also welcome a parent's joining him in retelling, over and over again, an enjoyable experience or even in acting it out. It should be a game mutually shared, rather than a performance the child is putting on before an admiring audience. Too much applause or too much pushing by the adult may give the child the idea that he is being cute and putting on a show—and this kills the idea of the activity's being simply a game, enjoyed for its own sake.

One form of directed dramatic play which may appear even in the nursery and kindergarten years is the use of pantomimic singing games such as those described in the chapters on dances. But even here the child should be encouraged to shape his own expression within the framework of the singing game and should not be expected to adhere to adult standards of skilled performance.

As children enter the primary grades, they are still vitally interested in spontaneous dramatic play. However this urge is often inhibited by such adult comments as, "Don't act silly!" "Be your age, Jimmy; you're seven now!" or "That isn't a gun! It's a broomstick." Often, too, the same subject matter that intrigued children of three and four may no longer challenge them; instead, they may be more likely to want to act out imaginative or fantastic stories, adventure tales, or realistic experiences they have observed or heard or read about.

During the age span of six through twelve, informal dramatics should be an extremely valuable and attractive part of each child's play life. Briefly, what are some of its specific purposes and values?

## Purposes of Informal Dramatics

This activity should help children gain ease in social cooperation through working closely with others in group dramatic play. It offers them the opportunity for controlled emotional release through which they may express many of the feelings which trouble them. Gradually they become more sensitive aesthetically, acquiring standards of good performance, respect for the discipline that must go into any art expression, and an early respect for the theater, whether as spectator or participant. They learn to think on their feet creatively and independently and gain ease in verbally expressing themselves. Through the playing of many roles they are better able to understand and appreciate those who are different from themselves. And finally, they have fun—in large doses!

## Role of the Adult Leader

As in other forms of play it is simply not practical or economical to have a trained dramatics leader working with tiny, informal groups of young children in a neighborhood setting. However, in schools or community centers skilled leadership can do much to direct this form of play into constructive and fruitful channels. If the dramatic experience is to reach its potential, the youngsters should meet with a leader fairly regularly; such a group may involve participation in a variety of integrated creative experiences or special focus on creative dramatics alone.

There is obviously no single best way to present dramatic play to children. Nonetheless, most leaders agree that certain types of activity are useful at the beginning. These include rhythmic activities and dancing, storytelling, musical play, and pantomimic and dramatic games.

*Creative Rhythms.* Through the sort of rhythmic play described in Chapter 8, the youngsters are helped to become relaxed and spontaneous, and to move expressively and imaginatively. In addition, they become accustomed to working as part of a unified group and enjoy wholehearted, unself-conscious participation. This includes the basic locomotor and axial rhythms, experiences with various types of rhythms and meters, spontaneous action to music or percussion accompaniment, and dramatization of songs and stories.

Boys in particular enjoy this kind of play when it is vigorous and physically challenging and, once they have come to accept it, do as well with it as girls. If they resist it at the outset, the leader may be wise to refer to it as acrobatic stunts, drills, or warm-ups, until they come to appreciate it for its own sake.

At the beginning a good part of the informal dramatic session with young children should be devoted to rhythmic expression; later on it may only be used occasionally or as an "ice-breaker" at the beginning of the session.

*Pantomimic Play.* After the children have explored sheer rhythmic movement for a period of time, they may be ready to concentrate on games or projects involving characterization or storytelling through movement. If they lack ideas or seem hampered by inhibitions, the leader may familiarize them with the idea of doing pantomimes by recalling to them television entertainers they have seen (such as Sid Caesar, Red Skelton, and others) who are expert in humorous pantomimes. Such clever and successful examples are likely to give them some respect for the activity and its possibilities. The leader may himself show some simple pantomimes such as milking a cow, climbing through a barbed-wire fence, driving a car, and the like. While the leader need not be an expert performer, it is important for him to show that this is an activity that gives an opportunity for real style and creativity and is not just to be done in a slapdash, thoughtless way.

Following this the leader may lead the children through some follow-the-leader sequences, with the above ideas or pretending to go on a trip (see the "Lion Hunt" in *Recreation Leader's Handbook*), or carry out other kinds of interesting pantomimes. Two possibilities are going through an amusement park and doing the various kinds of stunts available there (roller-coaster, shooting at targets, eating spun candy, etc.) or wandering through a toy factory and demonstrating the use of various kinds of toys.

Children may then pantomime other single actions, animals, toys, sports, hobbies, etc., until they have become familiar with this as an activity. One device the leader may use is to bring in an imaginary sack (Santa's sack). Each child in turn, takes something from the sack (an ice cream cone, a balloon, a fountain pen) and demonstrates (by licking it, blowing it up, or writing with it) just what it is. As each child performs, the other youngsters guess the meaning of his action.

*Mood Pantomimes.* From imitating the use of objects or showing familiar actions, children may progress to showing feelings or moods through movement. The leader may begin by initiating discussion of the different ways we feel at different times: happy, sad, angry, afraid, etc. He may ask the children to describe different times they remember when they felt one of these moods strongly. From this discussion may come examples of different moods and the happenings that provoked them. Then the leader may ask the children, all at once or one at a time, to pantomime these happenings and to show by their posture, facial expressions, and movements just how they felt when the events occurred.

EXAMPLES: *Fright.* A child is walking along a dark street late at night and hears footsteps coming up beside him. (He may be walking past a cemetery, for heightened effect). How does he show his feelings? What happens?

*Anger.* A child playing baseball is knocked down by another sliding into his base unnecessarily hard. What does he do?

*Surprise.* A child walks into his darkened living room. The lights go on and his friends rush out at him, laughing! It is a surprise birthday party.

Many other ideas will occur to youngsters for showing moods based on their own experiences.

A useful device for propelling an entire group into pantomimic expression of moods at once is to talk about how the movie director works. What are the words he uses as signals before the cameras begin to roll? *"Lights! Camera! Action!"* And what word does he use to stop the action? *"Cut!"* With these as cues the entire group of children may discuss a particular mood; then, at the proper signal, go into action. At *"Cut!"* they stop immediately. This tends to make a game out of the experience and to cut down on feelings of self-consciousness.

It is important in pantomimic play that children not be concerned about having to do what is "right" or what is "best." Just *doing* anything is the most important thing at first, and wholehearted encouragement and approval are important at this stage.

*Use of Voice.* In addition to physical expression, children may experiment with different ways of using their voices to convey ideas, moods, characters, and happenings.

Taking a simple, familiar phrase, such as "Hello," "What's this?" or "Come in," children may try saying it in different ways: excitedly, fearfully, happily, and lazily. When each child says the phrase (trying to convey his own interpretation), the others guess what he had in mind—and so it goes around the circle.

"Continued Story" is a useful game for this purpose. Children sit in a circle and spin a tall tale, with each child stopping at an appropriate point and then pointing to the next youngster at his right to continue. Exciting themes like pirates, haunted houses, sports, etc., lend atmosphere and interest, particularly if a child can take the part of different characters and use direct dialogue in telling his section of the story (which is, of course, completely improvised on the spot and unpredictable in outcome).

*Simple Incidents.* Children may then suggest simple incidents or happenings of a serious or humorous nature in which one youngster must play the key role—verbally.

Johnny is bringing home a bad report card. How does he approach his father?

Mary has found a wallet stuffed with hundred-dollar bills. What does she decide to do?

Sometimes the dialogue is clearly suggested by the nature of the part a child is attempting. Each one of the following characters has a fairly familiar line of chatter:

CIRCUS BARKER: "Come in, come in, come in! See the dog-faced boy! For one thin dime, tenth part of a dollar, see Grippo, the world's most powerful man . . ."

FOOTBALL COACH: "All right, men, it's half-time, and we're ten points behind. I want you to give all you've got for the old Alma Mater! Brown, hit that line as if you were a Mack truck! Jones . . ."

TELEVISION SALESMAN: "Here it is, the exciting new offer that you've been waiting for. It's a new vacuum cleaner, made by a famous company whose name I cannot . . ."

Children are likely to amaze the leader with their ability to parrot such lingo. While this is not creative in the sense of being a truly original expression, it is fun and tends to sharpen the child's powers of verbal characterization. Sometimes children may play simple verbal scenes in groups of three or four. Highly imaginative situations may be selected. "We're the first explorers to reach the moon on a space ship!" "Jim is running for President of the United States and he's just been elected." "We're a bunch of coal miners trapped in a mine shaft after the supports collapsed, and we're waiting for help . . ."

*Additional Stunts.* Before long children will be ready to take part in somewhat more demanding group stunts or skits. Various types of charade games in which they try to convey the idea of a book or movie title, famous saying, or character may be played. In addition, they may attempt "Prop Plays" or "Situation Skits," both described in *Recreation Leader's Handbook*.

*Prop Plays.* Children are given an envelope containing three or four diverse objects, which they are asked to blend into a little playlet.

EXAMPLES: Rubber dagger, shovel, lantern. "Two pirates land on a sandy shore at night. With a shovel, they dig a hole, to bury a treasure chest. One pirate then tries to stab the other with the dagger, to keep the treasure for himself. They fight. A lantern suddenly shines on them, and the shore patrol rushes up to arrest them both."

Apple, book, feather. "In a classroom, one child, while pretending to read a book, is tickling the youngster in front of him with a feather. The teacher sees this, and angrily asks the mischievous youngster to come forward. He does so, but quickly presents her with a big red apple. This might end peacefully—or, on the other hand, the apple might turn out to have a big worm in it, after the first bite."

*Situation Skits.* Children simply make up little skits about any situation, happening, or experience they are familiar with. Usually, such stunts turn out to be quite humorous.

*Skeleton Stories.* The children make up, or the leader gives them, a one-line plot. Dividing into groups, they then work out skits based on different interpretations or projections of the same one-line plot.

EXAMPLES OF PLOTS: You are in trouble, and someone helps you.

You are in a group of people or things that are all alike and you discover a stranger in your midst.

You discover a magic charm that gives you three wishes.

## Leadership Techniques

Throughout all such preliminary dramatic play the leader should encourage each child to participate through gentle encouragement and praise, and help when needed. As has been cautioned before, he should not attempt to impose adult values or standards but should try to bring out the child's honest response and expression. In a modified form the approach is one similar to "The Method" used in developing adult actors today, in which the individual tries to really *live* and *feel* the situation, rather than merely project or copy it outwardly.

This unself-conscious approach can best be achieved if the youngsters do not feel that they are on display, trying to get the applause and approval of others. The emphasis should be on sharing *with* others, rather than on acting *at* them. The setting should be an informal circular grouping in which interest shifts from one child to another, rather than a stage at one end of a room or hall with flat rows of chairs facing that end.

Although the leader does not impose his opinions, ideally, children will, through this dramatic experience, develop a deep sense of constructive criticism of the efforts of others; they will learn to judge who is really doing well and how each expression might be improved. Such is their interest and enthusiasm that those watching may often join in with noises, remarks, and spontaneous comments. While this sort of behavior would not be accepted in adult drama, it should be encouraged as a means of developing group sensitivity, involvement, and interest. Peter Slade comments, "Group intuition is no wild, unusual magic; but the adult reaches it only by discipline, the child only through freedom." [49] By the same token, when the group discusses what has happened, the leader should be careful not to offer his own positive ideas that will stifle individual comments and opinions.

While carrying on such informal dramatic play, children may enjoy improvising costumes for themselves; this adds to a feeling of realism and interest in the activity. However, costumes should not be permitted to become too elaborate or to interfere with grace or freedom of movement, and it is perfectly possible to carry on dramatic play with no special costumes. The same is true of properties, scenery, and stage settings; none of these are necessary to enjoyable play on this exploratory level. However, some dramatics leaders, such as Bette Butterworth, believe in having children design small "shoe-box" model sets as an early part of the play experience, thus broadening and deepening their involvement in the activity. And when the dramatic play extends to real performance, the making of costumes and sets becomes an important phase.

## Story Dramatization

After children have enjoyed such warm-up sessions, they may be ready to attempt a more ambitious project—either writing their own play or taking a story and working out their own dramatic version of it. Most successful leaders working in this field prefer to select a story that has the proper ingredients, and then have the children (with assistance) develop it.

What are the qualities of a good story for child dramatization?

1. It should be based on the interests and tastes of the group and should take into account their background, temperament, and experience. Where possible, it is a good idea to key it to seasonal or topical themes. This does not necessarily mean that it need be drawn from their immediate experience, since this would rule out fantasy, adventure, or happenings in other lands or ages as thematic material.

2. The story should not be too talky but should contain interesting action which can be readily shown. Ideally, it should contain a basic conflict which makes for suspense and interest. It is helpful if it is keyed to a single major theme which gives it artistic unity and direction, although there may be subplots or threads of action, of course. The plot should not be overlong, complicated, or rambling.

3. The characters involved should be individualized enough to allow for variety in their portrayal and should have a semblance of reality even if they are based on fantasy.

4. Most dramatics leaders agree that a story should contain a real mental challenge, a message of social value, and a socially desirable moral, although propaganda is certainly not a major purpose of the play experience.

*Introducing the Story.* After setting the mood for make-believe, the leader tells the story to the children, in a free, relaxed, friendly manner. He does not simply summarize it, but tells it with humor, mystery, suspense, and direct dialogue wherever possible. His exposition is clear and direct, and simplified only in so far as it is necessary to get across the main plot line. As he tells the story, and immediately after, he would discuss the meaning of the story and its various parts with the children. What was the most exciting moment in the story? Who were the important characters? How did the children like it, in general?

At this point it will become apparent whether or not the children really enjoyed the tale and would like to develop it dramatically.

The leader may have miscalculated its appeal for them. As an example, one leader, after children had spoken excitedly to him about having watched *Peter Pan* on television, began to develop it with them. It soon became apparent that they were not really interested in the story and that it would prove impractical for them in view of its reliance on different sets and technical devices, such as the invisible cable that enabled the star, Mary Martin, to fly about. Suddenly one child suggested that they act out *Davy Crockett,* which was then at its height of popularity. This met instant approval from all and proved to be a successful story theme.

Assuming that the children enjoy and want to follow up on the story the leader has told them, what happens?

They begin to discuss it in detail. Where does the story begin? When? What happens right at the start? Who are the important characters? How do they look and talk? Why do they act as they do? How much of the story can be acted out? Where would it end? What is the mood of the story?

In talking over the plot, children may establish a brief outline which will serve for a first play-through. Winifred Ward suggests that it may be helpful first to select characters on a trial basis and play it through without words, to establish the essential scenes and actions without having to worry about dialogue. Again they discuss the story and the way they have acted it out. At this point the leader may emphasize the dramatic content and conflict—as well as the climax. The children begin to better understand the relationships of the various characters and how the action develops the theme. The different scenes, entrances, exits, and stage action may come alive in greater detail. At all times, although the leader may have thought out solutions of his own, he should try to have the children arrive at their own creative decisions.

*Picking the Cast.* At some point children must be chosen to play different characters. They may volunteer to do this themselves, although it is then likely that certain more aggressive youngsters may carry off the plums. The leader may arbitrarily assign parts to youngsters, although this may be too directive an approach. Or he may ask the entire group, "Who do you think should play Ben? How about Mary," and so on. If the group is large enough, it may be divided into two or three separate casts each of which works on its own version of the play. Or it may be played through several times, with youngsters taking different roles each time. Then at the end, the children themselves might pick the cast they would like to have act it out in a final version.

*Dialogue.* The choice must also be made: should the dialogue be written, or taken directly from the play as found in a book, or should children simply adhere to the main lines of action and make up their own dialogue each time? There are advantages and disadvantages to each choice. Some children find greater security in playing a memorized role, while there is obviously greater creativity and stimulus to the imagination when children improvise their lines on the spot within a prestructured framework. The children themselves should make this decision and may use the "memorize" approach one time, and the "improvise" approach another time.

Again the youngsters act out the story. With the adult leader assisting or with a director chosen from their own group if they are mature enough, they then discuss it again. At this point they may go into finer details, such as enunciation and pronunciation of words, grouping and movement of the actors, and other shades of interpretation. If he is in the position of guiding this discussion, the leader should put the emphasis always on praise and encouragement. When specific comments are made regarding a particular role, they might be phrased in a nonpersonal way. Thus: "How about the way Long John Silver came in?" rather than, "Do you think Harry came in right?" When several casts act out the same story, comparisons might be made among the various treatments, not in a biting, unfavorable way, but from a constructive, helpful viewpoint.

After the final version of the play has been presented, either in their own small group or before a larger audience, the group would carry on a final evaluation in which its older members would be likely to play a key part.

"Was the story clear and understandable? Did it hold the interest of the onlookers?"

"Were the actors believable? Did they stay in character?"

"How was the dialogue? Was it realistic and interesting? Was it too short—or overlong?"

"How was the pace of the play, in general?"

"Did the players work as a team, reacting to each other, or were they a bunch of individuals making solo speeches?"

"Was the physical movement effective in contributing to the story?"

"What changes in the production might they make if they were to do it again?"

Other details of dramatic performance, having to do with such aspects as costuming, make-up, lighting, stage scenery, and management, are too technical for this text and are covered in books referred to in the bibliography. A final comment regarding this phase of informal dramatics might be that, if the play is to be shown to an audience, its most effective presentation is likely to be natural and unpretentious. If the audience sees it as the youngsters worked it out for their own fun, it will have much charm and appeal for them. If the production becomes too ambitious, they may view it through a pair of highly critical eyeglasses and it may not stand up.

## Children's Theater Activities

Often, interest in dramatic experiences for children extends beyond the casual, exploratory kind of program which has just been described to more formal and ambitious programs of children's theater. As the term is commonly understood today, this may mean either theaters in which adult actors entertain audiences of children or community theater ventures in which children themselves do the acting. In many cities and communities there have been successful examples of the latter, some of them quite impressive in scope.

The Palo Alto Children's Community Theater,[50] which began in 1932, grew in its first year from eight to 300 participants and in later years had as many as 1,000 children taking part in songs, dances, and pantomimes at special pageant programs. Subsidized by the city of Palo Alto, California, this venture had the following goals:

1. To create love of the beautiful through drama and the associated arts.

2. To afford entertainment and recreation for children of the city.

3. To provide a year-round indoor and outdoor program for all who were interested.

Children from six to sixteen were invited to participate; the most active ages were in the fifth- and sixth-grade levels. At every age children contributed according to their capacities. High school students headed the stage and lighting crews and make-up committees; junior high school children helped with those from intermediate grades, and intermediate grade youngsters with primary. Junior college students helped with all ages and did a certain amount of playwriting and direction.

Recognizing that all sorts of children were attracted to the children's theater program and for a variety of reasons, the directors saw counseling and the therapeutic aspects of the venture as being extremely important. Every effort was made to get a rich fund of knowledge about each participant through health records, sociological charts, notes of academic achievements, and informal chats. Every youngster, no matter what his individual problems or infirmities, was given as much place in the program as was possible.

Most of the plays put on by the Palo Alto Children's Theater were based on classical stories or fairy tales, such as *Robin Hood, Aladdin, Treasure Island, Cinderella,* and *Tom Sawyer.* Although its primary concern was theater, the participants were afforded many other experiences, such as dancing, choral work, handicrafts, puppetry, orchestra, and stagecraft.

Across the continent a somewhat different type of venture has developed in Westchester County, in New York State, under the leadership of the County Recreation Commission. The sequence of growth in dramatic activity began with a so-called "Children's World Theater," an adult performing group which toured summer playgrounds and gave theater-in-the-round performances for children. The success of this group led to the scheduling of a dramatics specialist on summer playgrounds and then to the formation of a summer Drama and Dance Center, which included art, music, and dance among its activities.

This then led to a winter Arts In Action Saturday morning workshop, and then to the formation of special Arts In Action units, to be held for ten-week periods, sponsored by local Parent-Teacher Associations. Bette Butterworth, Director of Dramatic Activities in Westchester County, explains that in today's streamlined homes in our growing suburban areas, modern children miss old-fashioned attics and basements, where pretending games, painting, and mess might reign supreme. Therefore the Arts In Action workshop strives to give children concentrated experiences in each of the creative mediums (art, puppet-making, dancing, rhythms, music) and then to combine them in single productions. Children may elect to take two activities during a single ten-week session and change their interests during the following session.

## Summary

This chapter describes the roles and purposes of dramatic play in the lives of children and outlines leadership techniques in developing pantomimic and verbal acting skills. Various devices for promoting dramatic play are presented, together with an analysis of the more ambitious type of "story-dramatization" project that may be carried on with regularly meeting groups. Two examples of community-wide children's theater programs are described.

# CHAPTER 11

# ENJOYING
# ARTS AND CRAFTS

Arts and crafts tends to be a less social form of play than the activities described in the previous chapters of this book. This is so because youngsters work, as a rule, on individual projects, in which they become deeply self-absorbed. There is another distinction, and that is that the product of an arts and crafts experience, simply because it is a tangible evidence of what has been done, assumes greater importance than the product of a game or dance session.

However, handicrafts form an essential part of a well-rounded play program for children simply because they are so attractive to many young-sters and because they draw upon another type of skill or ability. For youngsters who lack the qualities needed for success in the other forms of play that have been described, this activity may offer a real chance for success and prestige that they might otherwise be unable to achieve. And, in spite of its essentially individualistic nature, arts and crafts may be presented and worked with as a social experience with group instruction, projects, and other joint ventures.

Instead of placing art (as such) in one category and crafts in another, a modern concept would suggest that there is a broad field of creative activities in which all children may participate, making use of a variety of natural or manufactured materials and equipment, with which to develop creative and manipulative skills and organize and release their feelings about their physical and human environment. Thus the term refers not only to formal artistic and craft skills, but to all of a child's experiments with mud, clay, sand, crayons, pencils, chalk, scissors, paper and paste, finger paint,

189

and tempera and to his play with waste lumber, tin cans and bottles, pieces of wire, string and pipe cleaners, odds and ends of fabric, and the like.

When approached in this way, there is no clear-cut distinction between arts and crafts. A so-called craft, or construction project, should be approached as a truly expressive art experience, just as the designer and builder of a fine home or great bridge has both technical and aesthetic problems and opportunities. The skill, understanding, and creative pleasure that a child gains in one area are readily transferrable to another; from building a shack in the back yard to making linoleum-block Christmas cards; from constructing a puppet-show stage set to doing a crayon portrait of a friend.

Every parent, club leader, or classroom teacher who works with children in this area should have certain basic understandings, which are summarized in the following sequence:

He must realize that artistic experimentation and expressiveness is a natural and enjoyable attribute of each child. As part of his curiosity about life and his environment, he eagerly experiments with materials, manipulates toys and tools, and re-creates through graphic or plastic media, the things he sees all about himself. Call it art or not, these are the impulses that lead to early creative experiences.

Each child's form of expression is uniquely his own, and he should never be compelled to follow a model, to adhere to a common pattern for his age and sex, to do as well as the child beside him, or to copy adult art. Trying to impose such rigid standards is likely to stifle initiative, creativity, and enthusiasm in a youngster, just as a formal, stereotyped approach toward music with young children is likely to be self-defeating.

On the other hand, the interested adult should recognize that children go through certain broad stages or sequences of growth. These stages have been observed and recorded by authorities on child development, and they give us many clues as to the type of art experience children can best enjoy and profit from at any particular age, as well as the kind of expressions that are likely to ensue. Dr. Jack Arends, in his doctoral study, "Your Child Needs Art," [51] has outlined these stages in some detail. A few of his comments follow:

The preschool child is at first interested simply in exploring and enjoying materials for their own sake and for the sensations they give him. He scribbles haphazardly and places objects and toys at random, lacking muscular controls or highly organized plans. Usually he plays as an individual and is more likely to imitate the work of another than to collaborate with him on a joint project. At the age of four or five, with improving muscular skills and a greater knowledge of how to handle materials, the child carries on much drawing and construction play. He draws objects in a stylized way (circle for head, lines for arms and legs), gives names to what he has drawn, and may often tell a dramatic story about his pictures. He is not aware of relative proportions of parts of humans or other subjects and does not usually show perspective or background objects at all accurately.

At six, an age of wide interests and great diversity of play, the child draws human beings and animals in various settings and activities with a greater realism. He still uses crude conventions for showing perspective or distance, and makes arbitrary, unrealistic use of color, preferring vivid, warm tones. He has become much more capable with clay, cutting and pasting, simple weaving projects, and similar craft activities, and enjoys construction games like Tinker Toys, Erector Sets, and Lincoln Logs, although he rarely follows the manufacturer's suggested directions for projects.

At seven, youngsters work alone much of the time, are somewhat more selective in their interests, and have an increased interest span. Many youngsters find pencils preferable to crayon at this point since it enables them to work in greater detail, although the majority of children should still be encouraged to work "large," for which crayon is quite suitable. Children of this age take much pleasure in simple crafts and beginning forms of block printing, such as potato printing and stick printing. Eight-year-olds enjoy cooperating with each other in group enterprises and are much more capable of doing detailed and exacting work with soft pencils and colored crayons. Clay is still popular, and children of this age enjoy working with papier-mâché and other self-hardening materials. They take part in many forms of construction play and may even assist in carrying out simple repairs around the home.

Nine-year-olds have become much more analytical in their use of color and techniques of showing perspective, proportions, backgrounds, and surface decorations and textures. They can manipulate tools much more effectively and build surprisingly useful projects, often as coordinated group efforts. At ten and eleven, many children have developed drawing and painting skills that are quite impressive for their freedom, strength, and communicative value; on the other hand, many youngsters begin to lose interest in drawing or painting as such (possibly because with increasing age they have become subjected to more demanding standards of "does it look like?"). These children often begin to do much more with crafts, construction experiences, and similar technical hobbies, where they create surprisingly effective products.

With these understandings adults may ask, "How can I help children, at each stage of growth?"

## Adult Role in Arts and Crafts

Expressive play needs help and inspiration. Here are some of the ways in which parents or recreation leaders may encourage art expression:

*Providing Materials and Equipment.* Children should have plenty of opportunity to play with various kinds of natural materials (water, sand, mud, sticks, paper, boxes, cord, wire, construction blocks, and the like) as well as the more accepted kinds of art materials (finger paints, crayons, pencils, chalk, tempera and powder paints, clay and plastecine). These materials should be geared as closely as possible to their particular interests and stage of development, recognizing that some materials are useful over quite a span of years while others are more suitable for a particular age. Arnold Arnold, in his book *How to Play with Your Child,*[52] describes a detailed and helpful list of activities, toys, and arts and crafts materials which parents should make sure children have available from infancy through beginning adolescence.

In choosing such materials or toys, it is important to avoid the type of product which is already assembled or which a child simply puts together or operates according to a cut-and-dried formula and which allows little scope for his own self-expression. Many toys which are attractive and interesting to adults because they closely resemble the real thing (such as a miniature train or car) are of little sustained interest for children, because all they offer is the chance to push a switch or wind a key—and then sit back and be entertained. The preoutlined painting, in which a child must simply fill in the designated color in the spot marked by a certain number, is a sham—for two reasons. First, he is given no opportunity to express himself freely, and therefore the growth potential of the activity is limited. Second, such a project, just like the so-called "drawing lessons" which are occasionally seen on television, imposes an academic adult standard of performance which is very much unlike what the child would normally be doing at his age.

The same is true of craft materials. In recreation centers or summer camps, where pressure may be placed on the leader to have children produce objects to take home and show to their parents as evidence of what they have been doing, "pre-fab" projects may be used. Youngsters are taught to cut out doorstops, using stencils on wood, to saw off and polish plastic rings or bracelets, to knit whistle cords, or weave mats, which have no relationship to a child's sense of design, form, or self-expression. While these products may impress on a superficial level, they are not as valuable as truly creative projects.

In general, in selecting arts and crafts materials, it is desirable to use inexpensive materials (some of which can be concocted on the spot) as substitutes for more expensive materials. For young children particularly, the opportunity should be given to work "large," until their small-muscle capabilities have been refined. Crafts materials should be fairly durable, noncomplicated, scaled to the child's size (in the case of tools), and, obviously, safe to use. From a practical point of view, particularly when the workshop or art room has not been specially made for that purpose, it is best to use materials which do not make too much mess. As an example, crayon is much cleaner to use than chalk, which crumbles.

*Prividing Work Space.* Children need a space they can litter up freely, where there is real elbow room. A spot should be set aside, if at all possible, where they can store their art and construction materials, where they can be as noisy or messy as they please—but which they are responsible for cleaning up themselves. In the home, this may be in the basement, attic, or a corner of the garage. In a community center or camp, where fairly large groups of children must use the same work tables and equipment in turn, it is advisable to have special lockers or shelves to store work in progress and to have clearly understood responsibilities about maintaining equipment and cleaning up. This involves not just getting a floor and table surface clean, but keeping brushes, palettes, and mixing dishes in good condition, restoring tools to the proper place, throwing out waste materials, keeping clay moist, etc. Children who are untidy at home may learn habits of order and organization through this type of group responsibility.

*Providing Adult Understanding and Encouragement.* Although young children themselves do not usually place a high value on the specific object they have created (they often destroy it promptly and start over again), they appreciate an adult's concern and interest in what they are doing. Praise and encouragement are always welcome. The adult's questioning and comments, "That's an interesting line. How did you happen to do it?" or "Gosh, that's good color!" will stimulate and spur the child on. Too much emphasis on the youngster's turning out a fine piece of work as such may result in children's competing in their efforts for praise or attempting to copy adult pictures or objects.

As for adult understanding of the psychological factors underlying any particular expression, it is not wise for the average unskilled parent or teacher to attempt to delve too deeply. While those who are psychologically trained may learn much from the art expressions of disturbed children, it would be far too difficult and unreliable to attempt to interpret the paintings of most youngsters or to rely on these conclusions. Informal discussion of what lies behind a particular work may bring new understanding of the child's concerns and feelings and may heighten the warmth of an adult-child relationship, but this should be the limit in this direction.

*Guiding Technique.* Although he should not attempt to dominate the child's expression, there are occasions when an adult may help a child in his art experiences. This is particularly true when a new medium or project is being undertaken or when a child asks for help.

The parent or teacher may show how a paint is to be mixed, how the surface of paper should be prepared, how a cutting tool may be used safely, and how objects may be preserved in a workable state. By showing a new activity himself, he may interest and motivate youngsters toward it. Whenever he presents a particular skill in this way, he should be careful to reassure the child that what is most desired is not technical excellence, but the child's honest and enjoyable self-expression with the medium.

Finally, there are certain basic principles of art through which a product may be judged, having to do with form, composition, color harmonies, and the like. The intelligent parent or teacher who is unfamiliar with these will not attempt to teach them, but will leave them to the art specialist in the school or community center, who is equipped to do the best job with them.

Obviously a parent working with his own youngsters will find it much easier to operate in an informal way, encouraging them to experiment with their own choice of materials and on their own individual projects, than the leader or teacher who is working with a large group of children. The latter person will find it most practical to have special sessions or groups of sessions devoted to the exploration of single activities, such as finger painting, soap carving, block printing, and the like. This simplifies the use of space, the preparation and care of materials, the storing of work, and similar problems. It also means that when he demonstrates techniques, all of the children at once may share in this learning experience. This does not imply that the goal is uniformity of expression. Within the broad framework of using the same materials, each child is free to develop his own particular project or experiment, while the leader, in moving around the room, is free to give each individual whatever degree of help or direction he seems to want or need.

How does this work? In crayon drawing, for example, the leader may supply children with the needed paper and crayons and then may demonstrate the various ways in which the crayons may be held and used. He may then suggest that the children experiment themselves and, after a time, see what kinds of effects they have created. Here there is no suggested theme or framework—simply exploration. Within a few moments the children are likely to show examples of:

LINES: straight, curved, zigzag, spiraling

TEXTURES: stippled, cross-hatched, solid tones

GEOMETRIC FORMS: circles, triangles, squares, rectangles

OBJECTS: while some children will be nonobjective, others, even without being urged to do so, will probably have drawn recognizable forms.

The leader might talk over all of these forms of expression with the children and, in addition, might comment, or ask for their reactions, on the way color has been used and on the types of compositional effects that were achieved. Even at this early stage certain principles of composition might be suggested by the leader, assuming that he is somewhat familiar with them. If the children have taken part in creative rhythms and have developed their own dance forms, this experience might logically be tied to that.

In moving along to further experiences, the leader might encourage the children simply to experiment further with the materials—or he might aid some who are lacking in inspiration by having the group discuss experiences or subjects which might provoke interesting drawings. Trips to the zoo, the circus, a factory; stories they have seen on television; books they are reading—anything of this kind may suggest subject matter. The stimulus may be as broad as a discussion of moods, as in creative dance, or, if it appears advisable, as narrow as a still-life grouping the children set up themselves as a model.

At a logical point the leader might encourage the youngsters to examine each other's work, drawing out their reactions and offering his own in a tactful, helpful way. If he wishes to do so and if he feels that the children are ready for it, he may use the work of different youngsters to illustrate the principles of perspective, proportion, composition, and the use of lines and colors that were touched on earlier. However, throughout this process he should stress that the most desired qualities are those of freshness and imagination. Vigorous, honestly childlike pictures that are strong in color, storytelling, and decorative effects are to be preferred to those which show a precocious mastery of academic draftsmanship or technique in the use of art materials.

Some questions that the adult might suggest at this stage are:

"Does the picture make a pleasing pattern in the way it combines shapes, colors, lines, and textures?"

"Does it make good use of the space available? How does it appear when seen from a distance—top-heavy, or lop-sided, or well-balanced?"

"Is there a unity to the picture—or is it a haphazard scattering of different ideas and images?"

"What is it trying to say—and how well does it say it?"

In appraising any such example of child art the adult should recognize that distortion in terms of forms or proportions is to be expected at this age, and often has a logical basis in that the child views certain objects or parts of a picture as being more significant than others. This viewpoint is something he shares with primitive artists and many respected modernists; therefore the whole question of realistic and accurate presentation of forms is something that must be carefully handled.

## Other Projects

The same type of approach may be used with various kinds of construction and craft projects ranging from the very simplest to the most complex. Such ventures include the making of stage sets, mobiles (hanging assemblies of paper, wire, wood, and other objects), collages (compositions employing paper, wood, stones, etc, in paste-up form), group murals or designs, group picture newspapers or class magazines, textile patterns, or posters for group events.

The children themselves may do much to determine how long they should stay with a particular medium or project, but it is up to the leader, whether the group be large or small, to help them establish time limits, to determine when they have gone about as far as they can with a certain project, and to suggest new kinds of ventures they can attempt. And even in a large group, when certain class or club hours are set aside (as has been described) for group exploration of a single medium, it is possible to schedule a certain amount of free time when children can work on whatever type of project they are interested in—be it in any area at all.

## Summary

This chapter discusses the role of arts and crafts in the play program of children and describes certain broad stages of participation and basic principles of adult leadership of art activity. The need for providing equipment, materials, work space, and adult understanding and encouragement is outlined, and certain techniques for guiding group sessions in this form of activity are presented.

# CHAPTER 12

# OTHER ACTIVITIES

NATURE STUDY AND CAMPING, GARDENING AND

PET CARE, HOBBIES AND COLLECTING

Another highly rewarding form of play experience is the type which is concerned with nature study and the skills of camping and outdoor living. There are many reasons why this sort of recreational activity makes a unique and important contribution to the growth of children.

Simply living out of doors for a short period of time is a valuable kind of experience for youngsters who live in cities or in crowded suburbs where there are no uncluttered fields and woods to play in.

> Children need relief from the pressures of modern, adult society. . . . The tenseness and bustle of life in an industrial nation is not an ideal child growth climate. Children need at least occasional relief from it in a relaxed, free environment where facilities, program, and personnel are tailored to child size and tempo.[53]

In recent years many communities have recognized this need and, through their school systems, have initiated school camping programs, beginning with about the fifth or sixth grade and continuing through secondary school. Partly this is because they recognize the fact that nature experiences have a unique appeal for children because of our national heritage. "The American tradition is an outdoor tradition. We look back with pride to our rugged pioneer background, in which the explorer, the Indian, the frontiersman, the settler, the trapper . . . played such prominent and heroic roles."[54]

Camping recreation often involves strenuous activity, another reason

198

for its special value at a time when it has been estimated that American children spend over 90 per cent of their time either sitting (in cars, at meals, and in school) or lying down and when surveys have indicated that the average youngster watches the equivalent of a full-length movie show each day on television.

A final, crucial factor in the appeal of this form of activity is that children in the preadolescent years, on the threshold of taking responsible roles in society, enjoy real jobs and experiences, rather than theoretical or artificial learning projects. They want to go places, to see and do things. Becoming identified with team projects and activities, preparing and improving camp sites, doing their own cooking and cleanup, being of service to the community through conservation work and wildlife maintenance—all these are direct, first-hand experiences which make them doubly fun.

Whether camping programs of this sort are administered by schools, public or private camps, community recreation agencies, or, on a much smaller scale, as part of family vacation periods, there are many specific kinds of activities which children in the preteen group may carry on.

## Nature Study

Children may collect and press leaves, flowers, and plants. They may find and identify larval and adult insects, snakes, rodents, birds, and other forms of forest life. They may study ant and bee colonies, learn about various types of soil and rock formations, experiment with weather observation and prediction—and in general gain an understanding of the world of nature (and the relation of man to it) that would be quite impossible if they were not in such a setting.

In terms of man's role, they may be guided in various types of conservation, wildlife control and reconstruction activities. This may include improving the camp facilities by building trails, dams, and footbridges as well as actually assisting in the construction of camp buildings. They may clear brush, plant new trees, erect bird-feeding stations, and construct game shelters. They may build and improve new aquatic facilities: beaches, docks and floats.

When the camping experience is conducted by a school, certain types of learnings may be emphasized through integration with activities that are normally offered as part of the school's program:

*Science.* This is the most obvious form of correlation and is one reason why it is often recommended that science instructors be placed in charge of camping programs. Biology, astronomy, chemistry, and various other areas of science come into constant play in the child's hour-by-hour experiences in such a camp.

*Art.* There are many opportunities for children to sketch trees, flowers, and animals, to make charts and maps of camp areas, to make signs labeling trees and camp areas, to construct papier-mâché models of the camp terrain, to make splatter leaf-prints, and the like.

*Language Arts.* Children may be encouraged to keep notebooks and diaries recording their experiences and to put up bulletin boards when back at school, recounting their adventures. They may produce a daily, mimeographed camp newspaper. They may make up lists of new words encountered in their travels to use in discussions and reports later on. They may write stories and poems about the camp session—either specific happenings or, in a more general way, their impressions of the sights, sounds, and sensations that were new to them.

*Practical Conservation.* They become familiar with practices in land maintenance, forestry, trapping, and fishing.

*Health and Safety.* They should be given effective briefing sessions on recognition of dangerous insects, snakes, and plants and should become thoroughly familiar with the rules of water safety and techniques of first aid. They should learn the practices of safe fire management so thoroughly that they will never as adults contribute to the tremendous toll this nation suffers each year from thoughtlessly set forest fires. They should learn forest survival skills, what to do when lost, how to find safe water and edible plants, and how to protect themselves from the elements.

*Homemaking Skills.* At home the idea of purchasing and preparing food for meals may seem sissy for many boys. In the forest this activity assumes a real challenge, and boys and girls may share this important task with pleasure and a growing respect for each other.

There are many other aspects of camping life. Children may take special hikes and trips to explore a historically interesting region, to examine different kinds of terrain, or to visit farms or other kinds of rural occupations. In terms of historical understanding, they may find out about the first settlers of the region, what its role was during different historical periods of the country, and similar topics. They may put their mathematical skills to work by estimating food needs and costs in advance of the trip, miles covered in travel, time spent in various enterprises, and measurements needed for construction or other work about the camp.

While all of these experiences may appear, at first view, to be far from play—as it is popularly conceived of—the fact is that they are dramatic, exciting, and pleasurable and therefore are worth being considered as recreation. And, of course, in the evenings and at other periods during the day there should be plenty of opportunity for games, sports, dancing, singing, and other forms of relaxed play.

## Camping Guides

When the camping setting is a fairly wild one, certain basic rules may be suggested:

*Shelter.* There is a considerable range of types of shelters that may be set up, depending on the degree of comfort desired, the length of the camping expedition, and the expense that the campers are willing to go to. Various types of windbreaks, or brush or tarpaulin lean-tos may be erected quickly and inexpensively. Tents, such as the umbrella, wall, pup, mountaineer tent, or tepee, provide varying degrees of comfort. When a tent is pitched, it should be placed on a level spot, free of projecting tree roots or large boulders and not directly under trees with large dead limbs, in case of a windstorm.

The tent should be erected so it is taut and wrinkle-free; after it is erected, a ditch should be dug around it to carry off surface drainage or rainfall. At the lowest point of the ditch a trench should be dug to carry the water away. The camp site should be close to a supply of drinking water and firewood, although if the campers are using a gasoline, kerosene, or alcohol stove, it may not be necessary to have a wood fire.

*Protection from Pests.* The bottom of the tent should be made absolutely tight to keep snakes out, and it is advisable, if there are many insects around, to spray the area around the tent with DDT or other insecticides each night. All food should be kept in vacuum jars or other tight containers and, if necessary, hung from trees, to keep it safe from ants or other animals. Lights should be used as little as possible after dark, in order not to attract insects. All garbage and table leavings should be buried, burned, or disposed of at least a hundred yards away from the tent site, for they will tend to attract unwelcome forest visitors.

*Sanitation and Safety.* All drinking water should be screened through a clean, closely woven, white cloth to remove particles or organisms. If possible, water should be traced to its source to make sure it is not a swamp or other unhealthy drainage area. If there is any doubt about its purity, it should be thoroughly boiled and then cooled for drinking or cooking purposes, or one of the new drugs, such as halazone, used to purify it.

All mushrooms should be avoided, unless the campers are very sure of the appearance of edible forms. Pokeweed and other poisonous berries or fruits should be known, as well as the edible forms of wild berries. Matches should never be left loose, or they may be taken by mice back to their nests, a dangerous source of fire. In woods inhabited by snakes snakebite kits and antivenom serum should be part of the camp's equipment, and the campers should be familiar with methods of treating snake bite. Safety procedures relating to being lost in the forest, building and extinguishing fires, water and firearms safety, and building emergency stretchers should all be part of the precamp briefing.

*Fires and Cooking.* Campers should be familiar with the basic rules for building fires, and should know the various types: council fire, reflector oven, star fire, hunter-trapper, pyramid fire and others. They should know which types of wood are suitable for the different purposes to which a fire may be put and should be able to use an axe, hatchet, or knife safely and efficiently in building fires.

Camp cookery need not be complicated, but is an important part of the camp experience; youngsters should know how to bake vegetables, meat, or fish, to make pancakes, stew, eggs, and various kinds of hot drinks and other recipes under fairly primitive conditions.

There are a number of excellent sources which cover these skills in detail; these are listed in the bibliography at the end of this book.

## Gardening and Pet-care Projects

Closely allied to the sort of nature study that is carried on during camping expeditions are gardening and pet-raising ventures which may be attempted closer to home.

At a comparatively early age children may assist parents in caring for flower beds or vegetable gardens, and by the age of seven or eight they may be ready to maintain their own small plots. If there is land available close by, they may help to prepare the soil, plant seeds, cuttings, or young plants, and cultivate the land by weeding, fertilizing, and watering it. In time they are able to harvest the flowers, fruits, or vegetables that come from their efforts and to contribute these to the family larder or flower decorations.

At first only simple projects should be attempted, under fairly close adult direction. As youngsters gain in skill and understanding, they learn to decide what to plant, to establish a sequence of flowering or harvesting through the growing season, and even to experiment with plant propagation (as a number of school systems have done with elementary school youngsters) by rooting cuttings or doing air layering with shrubs and young trees. Older children, if they are successful, may actually go into this as a form of beginning business enterprise, by selling their produce at roadside stands or supplying markets or resorts with their crops if they are in sufficient quantity.

This type of enterprise lends itself to large groups of children in schools or camps and to one or two at a time in home settings. Even in the city, where there is no land as such, children may be responsible for window boxes and indoor planting, using the type of plant supplied by florists or even planting potatoes, onions, grapefruit, and the like for the leafy foliage they afford.

## CARE OF PETS

Many children also enjoy caring for pets—either the customary dog or cat—or animals which may be their own special responsibility, such as rabbits, white rats, guinea pigs, or domestic birds. Through this type of experience they can gain a richer understanding of life's processes and learn to take responsibility for living creatures which are dependent on them—just as they are dependent on their own parents.

Pet-care projects of this kind are also fairly common in schools, since children are there daily and can arrange to take animals to their homes over weekends or holidays. (Pets like turtles, snails, newts, and some aquarium fish, which can live without daily care, might safely be left at school over weekends.) Clubs which meet weekly or less often are not as well suited to this type of activity; nor are summer camps, unless arrangements can be made to have the pets boarded during the months of the year when the camp is not in session.

For the child who lives in the country, such projects are a normal prelude to his later joining such organizations as the 4-H clubs or Future Farmers, when he will, as a matter of course, go into agricultural ventures of a much more elaborate nature. But, if anything, they are of even greater value for city and suburban youngsters who do not normally see natural life all about them and who do not have the opportunity for close-up experiences with dependent living things.

## Collections and Hobbies

Once again, the term "collections and hobbies" describes activities which tend to be carried on individually, rather than by large groups of youngsters. This is not necessarily a fault; children often need time to be alone, rather than constantly in the thick of group activities and pressures. This is a time when a child may be by himself, reflective, peaceful, exploring his own special interest and developing an area in which he has a unique competence, knowledge, and skill. Other reasons why collecting or carrying on hobbies are valuable is that the child does not *need* the group to have fun with them, and that he may carry them on beyond the age of childhood through adulthood. President Roosevelt had an extensive stamp collection which afforded him many moments of pleasure and relaxation, and Winston Churchill's hobby of landscape painting has often been publicized.

In a sense, the separate words, "hobby" and "collection," are often synonymous; a child's collection may be his hobby, and vice versa.

Any deep-seated continuing interest may be classified as a hobby. It is needless to name all the possible ones: chemistry, construction of model planes, trains, and boats; ham radio; various types of music activity; gardening—in fact, many of the activities that have been described earlier in this book.

The list of possible kinds of collections is equally long and diverse: autographs, stamps, coins, leaves, dolls, match books, sea shells, mementoes of travel, playbills and tickets to shows, photographs—and hundreds more.

A parent may help a child in carrying on a hobby or collection in several ways.

First, he may assist him in organizing it practically. Where can he get information on the subject? Where can he get supplies and equipment, in the case of a hobby? How can he set up a scrapbook, display case, or files or shelves, in the case of collections? Parents can help children find some of the answers that do not come too readily to young minds—and children can take it from there. An excellent source of free ideas, publications, and opportunities is the recently published *A Wonderful World for Children,* by Peter Cardozo,[55] which lists many albums, atlases, books, brochures, catalogues, films, games, guides, how-to magazines, manuals, maps, samples, and services. Surprisingly, many companies and government agencies distribute a wealth of such aids, and parents who wish to help their children enrich their hobby life can make good use of this concentrated listing of them. A few samples:

Free stamps and stamp albums for beginning collectors

Booklets on chemistry, carpentry work, model railroading, astronomy, gardening, music, model cars, soap carving, knot tying, and many others

Educational comic books, natural history "libraries," magazine subscriptions, games, card tricks and magic tricks, calendars, picnic plans, and the like

Shooting lessons, rifle targets, and dog-training books

Information on many contests, organizations, and sports activities

Posters, paintings, maps, and recipes

While many of these are simply commercial releases which serve to advertise a particular product and would be of little use to children, many others would be genuinely helpful and informative for them to have. There are many other useful books describing various useful hobbies for parents and children; a recently published one is *Hobbies for Pleasure and Profit,* by Horace Coon.[56]

It goes without saying that, particularly for parents and their own children, there is always the happy prospect of becoming joint partners in a mutual enterprise. This is not a good idea if the parent takes up the hobby simply to be with his youngster, in a sacrificing frame of mind— but there are many intriguing activities or collecting "bugs" which are suitable for various ages and which parents and children can share.

The schoolteacher or recreation leader who works with larger groups of children obviously cannot share interests with each of these youngsters. However, he can help them organize "Hobby Fairs," exhibitions for which children may bring in and demonstrate their hobbies. Sometimes it may simply involve exhibitions of collections; sometimes it may involve performances of card tricks, magic stunts, etc.; sometimes it may be a pet-judging contest—but there are many possibilities. School assemblies and interclass parties may easily be built around hobbies in this way.

## Summary

This chapter has briefly described additional play activities which many children enjoy in the areas of nature study, camping, gardening, and pet-raising, and hobbies and collecting. Suggestions are given to adults who wish to encourage and guide children in these pursuits, with several sources of useful information.

# CHAPTER 13

# SPECIAL EVENTS
# AND PARTIES

In any sustained recreational program for children, there is a need for occasional special events or parties which are out of the ordinary and which provide a special highlight and excitement. Children look forward to this type of event with great enthusiasm and remember it long afterward if it has been successfully planned and carried out.

When children have been taking part in music, drama, dance, or art activities, it makes sense to have a culminating event, which may take the form of a recital, demonstration, or exhibition. Such final shows should not be too formal or place too much stress on perfectionism. Instead, they should simply be relaxed and pleasant opportunities to review the experiences the children have had together and to see some of the outcomes of these experiences. Some extra preparation should be devoted to culminating events, during the weeks preceding a show; motivation and interest are likely to be heightened during this period, and there need be no fearful anticipation or worried suspense unless that is the attitude of the adult leader. In a sense, a final demonstration seems to tie the whole experience up in a neat package, putting the cherry on top of the sundae—if it is well done.

Special events need not come only at the end of a series of meetings.

Summer playground directors often plan them on a weekly basis, in addition to the regular activity program. Thus every Wednesday afternoon children will know that there will be a special show, contest, or party of some kind—which will be publicized by posters, announcements, and stunts of various kinds. Here are some typical examples:

*Costume parties.* Children dress up; prizes may be awarded for most unusual costumes, etc.

*Pet shows.* Children bring various kinds of pets, and awards are given to the most unusual, handsomest, largest, smallest, oldest, youngest, etc.

*Hobby shows.* Children may demonstrate collections, products of arts and crafts work, photographs they have taken, airplane or boat models, etc.

*Field days.* Various kinds of track and field events for older children, with novelty stunts or self-testing activities for the younger ones; this may be ended by a short softball game or other such feature.

*Tournaments.* During a single afternoon, tournaments of table tennis, shuffleboard, horseshoe throwing, deck tennis, dart throwing, or checkers may be held.

*Trips.* The director may schedule several trips during the summer, to nearby ball parks (which often have children's days at special rates), beaches, amusement centers, museums, or zoos, with volunteer parents accompanying the group.

There are many other kinds of possibilities, including carnivals, fiestas, and parties with special themes. This type of special event requires much planning and organization if it is to be a success. Ideally it should involve as many children as possible in active participation and should be an important force in stimulating playground attention and making each youngster's summer experience alive and interesting.

## Parties

There are many occasions for having parties, whether children are at home or in community centers, clubs, or at school. As a rule there is some special reason for giving a party—such as a birthday, holiday, or other special purpose.

When the party is being held for very young children up to the age of seven or eight, it should be quite simple and fairly brief. It need not have any special theme and should not (especially for preschool youngsters) have much in the way of organized activities. Here are several guides for home parties or *small* parties in other settings:

*Supervision.* It is important to have enough adults present. In a home party this might mean one parent for every five or six children present. With a larger group it might be one adult for every ten children. If children are under the age of six, it will be all right to have only mothers or women leaders present. If they are older and of both sexes, it is a good idea to have men present, to maintain a reasonable amount of control and to handle any emergencies that might arise that might require a masculine touch.

A good rule of thumb as to the number of children to invite to a party is to invite one for each year of the "birthday" child. Five guests are enough for a five-year-old, or ten for a ten-year-old. A number of similar helpful suggestions were offered in a picture series dealing with children's parties, recently published by *Life* magazine.[57]

*Refreshments.* These should be plentiful, easy to serve, and attractive to children. Doughnuts that may be bought in quantity and ice cream cups or sticks are far superior to anything that must be specially cooked and served warm—such as frankfurters or hamburgers. If expense is a matter of concern, punch mixes like Hi-C or Kool-Aid are excellent; otherwise, bottled soda pop or apple cider usually appeal to children, as do the various frozen fruit concentrates now available. There are many special recipes for preparing tempting and attractive spreads, but, for the most part, this effort and expense is wasted, since children don't appreciate lavish effects. It is a good idea to serve at only one or two fixed times during a party and within a limited area or space. This will keep down horseplay, throwing food around or popping paper cups on the floor, etc. This kind of roughhousing is dangerous both to clothes, and to life and limb when children start to slide across a wet floor. When parties are run in a formal way, often by dancing schools, there is the practice of having each boy bring refreshments to his seated partner, but for most youngsters this would be an artificial and stilted procedure.

*Decorations.* Usually very simple decorations are sufficient, placed strategically at the entrance and at the table where refreshments are being served. Crepe paper, balloons, and streamers help to create a party atmosphere, and, if it is a small birthday party, paper hats and other favors are also useful. For large parties of older children, particularly when there is a special theme, decorations may be somewhat more elaborate and may include such objects as corn shocks, pumpkins, paper hearts, flags, shamrocks, etc. (as in some of the suggested party programs to follow).

*Activities.* There are many traditional games, such as Pin the Tail on the Donkey, Musical Chairs, and others included in Chapter 6 of this book, which children enjoy playing at parties. When there is a large group present, and when boys tend to be overwild in an effort to show off before girls (parties are very stimulating), it is wise to have a considerable amount of time devoted to organized games and comparatively little time for free play. Group singing is an excellent activity, as are folk and square dancing (ballroom for older children if they have had some instruction in it). It is not wise to attempt to teach any new activities at the typical party. If there is planned entertainment such as a magician, films, or other acts, it should not continue long enough for children to be bored. While passive entertainment of this kind is not normally the best form of recreation for children, sometimes it represents the easiest way out for the harassed adult at a children's party. A word of caution is not to have the party overlong; when children start to show their exhaustion by being wild, *it's over*! Between one and two hours is usually sufficient.

### Party Themes

For older children a party is likely to have more unique interest and appeal if it has a special theme and if the various elements of the party—such as refreshments, decorations, and activities—are cued to this theme. Here are several examples of such themes which are most suitable for preteen parties:

*Shamrock Party* (for St. Patrick's Day). The invitation and publicity posters are in the form of shamrocks (made from green paper). Shamrocks, green balloons and streamers, and pictures of the Emerald Isle, which may be obtained from travel or steamship agencies, are used as decorations. Party activities may include doing Irish songs and dances, playing games based on the Blarney Stone or on relays with Irish potatoes, or playing a variation of Dizzy Izzy (page 56), turning on an improvised shillalagh. As another stunt children may be given paper, Scotch tape, etc., with a prize going to the youngster who makes the best Irish costume for himself.

In this, as in several of the following parties, games must be revised or altered in order to have them seem to fit the theme. Often the adult leader will not find ready-made materials for the program, and must therefore use his own ingenuity and the ideas of the children to work out activities that fit the subject.

*St. Valentine's Day Party.* Invitations and decorations make use of motifs of a red paper heart and of Cupid shooting off his little bow and arrow. Red and white streamers may be used in decoration, and heart-shaped cookies may be part of the refreshments. Children are supplied with colored paper and paste and scissors to design their own valentines. As a novelty, each child may be asked to compose a valentine; these may be placed in a pile, with each youngster then choosing and reading one. Various pairing-off games may be played; children thus take partners, either for dancing or, if they are not at this stage, simple games which also make use of a heart as a prop. One example is Cardboard Relay (page 56), with red cardboard hearts. Another variation of a familiar theme might be, Pin the Arrow on the Heart. Familiar songs that belong to the occasion, such as "Let Me Call You Sweetheart," might also be sung.

*Hallowe'en Party.* There are many possible names for a party given on this colorful holiday, such as "Goblin's Gambol," "Pumpkinhead Party," or "Graveyard Rendezvous." The Hallowe'en theme is carried out in the invitations, publicity, and decorations, with plenty of black cats, broomstick-riding witches, and pumpkins; orange and black colors predominate. Ducking for apples and fortunetelling are traditional stunts at this time, as well as blindfold games. Children may wear masks and wigs and are likely to enjoy telling ghost stories with all the lights turned out but a single guttering candle inside a pumpkin. Another possible stunt is to have one room or hallway leading to the party converted into a "Chamber of Horrors" with faint, blinking, red lights, clanking chains, and an electric buzzer and wild shrieks going off, etc. When this stunt is arranged by teenagers or adults, it is common to give those going through the darkened room objects to handle (such as peeled grapes, telling them these are the eyes of a slain victim), but this is far too gruesome for children. Great care should be taken not to have any of the activities too frightening or stimulating.

*Patriotic Party.* A party of this kind may be planned for any national holiday that has patriotic significance, such as a birthday of one of the famous presidents, and may specifically be titled "Washington's Birthday Ball," etc. The invitations may be set against a background of a flag, tiny outlined shape of the United States, or little red hatchet (cherry tree incident), and decorations would naturally emphasize red, white, and blue bunting. Children might sing patriotic songs such as "Yankee Doodle" or "Dixie," and might do traditional old American dances such as the Virginia Reel. Quizzes about famous events of American history might be given, and teams could be formed (North and South, or by favorite states) to compete in such contests as solving jumbled names on a list of famous Americans or identifying the authors of famous quotations. This sort of party would be more effective for children who have had some American history in their schoolwork.

*Toss-and-Bounce Party.* In this type of party children would play various skill games, such as tossing quoits over the legs of an up-ended chair, dropping clothespins into a milk bottle, bouncing a tennis ball into a pail set on a chair, sailing paper plates through a hoop suspended from the ceiling, or trying to ring a suspended bell by throwing a beanbag at it. These and similar games may be found in Chapter 6. Children may play them individually (each youngster with his own scoreboard) or may circulate from event to event in small teams that compete against each other.

The ideas for the preceding parties and some of the activities described came from *The Party Book,* by Mary Breen.[58] This book includes many other party themes, such as "Dude Ranch Rodeo," "Comic-strip Party," "County Fair," "A Mexican Fiesta," and others. For the most part these are either too advanced for children of this age or too expensive and time-consuming to be worth the effort. However, they contain many useful and interesting ideas, and prospective party-givers would do well to look over this book and discuss the possibilities it contains with the children the party is to be given for—as an aid to planning a really bang-up event.

Another excellent source of new and unique ideas is the *Recreation Program Aids,* published by the National Recreation Association.[59] This is a bimonthly folder which contains descriptions of many program activities in the areas of sports, arts and crafts, dramatics, music, games, and special events. It also offers free brochures and materials having to do with all phases of recreation programming including party outlines, decorations, and recipes, etc. It is particularly valuable because much of its content is fresh and catchy and because it is usually attuned to the weeks and months lying just ahead. Thus the leader or parent receiving the program aids bulletin in January would find many activities and ideas suitable for the winter and early spring months—just when he is planning ahead for this period.

## Summary

This chapter deals with culminating activities and special events as part of a children's play program. In some detail it analyzes the procedure of giving parties and suggests several specific party themes which are suitable for older children.

# CHAPTER 14

# FAMILY FUN

In recent years the slogan has often been heard, "The family that prays together stays together."

This might readily be paraphrased to, "The family that *plays* together stays together."

Decades ago when most American families lived in rural areas or in rambling homes on quiet, tree-lined streets (with members of several generations all together), there was a much stronger sense of family structure and "belongingness" than we have today. Broken homes, outside pressures and attractions, the hectic pace of modern living, and the fact that so many fathers must commute to work mean that too many children do not see their parents as much as they should. There is a great need to plan for more recreational activities that parents and children can carry on together —not just occasionally, but regularly, and in many forms of play.

This has already been discussed at some length in Chapter 3, but it is interesting to note what children themselves have to say. According to a well-known psychiatrist,[60] happy, well-adjusted youngsters have this to say about their home environments:

1. Parents listen to and accept the child's early ideas and ambitions.
2. Parents do things *with* him and not just *for* him.
3. Parents tell stories to children.
4. Parents laugh and joke with the youngsters.
5. The family does a lot of things together.
6. Parents give children "real" things to do; this makes them feel mature and responsible.

In his excellent book, *The Family Scrapbook,*[61] Ernest Osborne points out that often parents take their job of raising children so seriously that

213

they get no fun from living with them. "It's a good idea . . ." he suggests, "to replace some of the concern about our children's development with sheer enjoyment of them." Instead of always being grown-up and stuffy, parents should let down their hair and relax, sometimes permitting themselves to be foolish and whimsical. There should be plenty of time for talking things over, for having family jokes, and—for doing things together.

Many of the activities listed earlier in this book lend themselves readily to parents and children playing together. They include:

Sharing hobby interests; sailing, fishing, hiking and camping; arts and crafts fun; photography; collecting; trips and outings; family dramatic enterprises; family music (record-listening, playing instruments and singing, and concert-going); folk and square dancing (particularly with older children); outdoor cooking; active and social games and mixers; and many others. There is literally no form of wholesome recreation that families cannot in some degree share, and there are very few places in the home where some kind of recreational activity cannot be carried on.

It is not sufficient simply to provide toys and equipment to children. They want to participate *with* their parents and to share the "togetherness" that this can help to bring about.


## Taking Stock

Larry and Helen Eisenberg, outstanding recreational authorities who have done much leadership training for the Methodist church throughout the country, have organized a fine collection of materials in *The Family Fun Book*.[62] In it they suggest that families should take inventories to see what their play interests are and what new ones they might develop:

1. Make up a list of hobbies and other activities.

2. List all the physical facilities in the home which may be used for family play, living room, dining room, kitchen, playroom, basement, fireplace area, yard, outdoor play area, etc.

3. Do the same for the community, parks, bowling alleys, swimming pools, movies, schools, churches, clubs, etc.

4. List the recreational equipment the family owns or could get.

5. Determine what daytime or evening hours might be available for family fun. This would not have to result in a rigid schedule; however, it helps to know that during the last three weeks in July the family will be

able to plan an extended auto trip, and that on certain evenings of the week or on Saturday afternoons everyone is free for joint activities.

After discussing the interests the family members share in common and the other factors of time, place, and equipment, a tentative schedule or plan for expanding and enriching family play might be developed. This might be made into an informally decorated calendar and placed on a bulletin board in the kitchen or playroom. Such a plan might have several chief emphases:

1. Making fun out of routine activities
2. Developing common recreational interest, in general
3. Having regular family nights when all may enjoy the same hobbies or activities, or each individual the activity he is most interested in and when games may be played and other special stunts carried on
4. Getting the most out of back-yard fun
5. Carrying on outings and trips or camping expeditions
6. Having special family parties with guests and visitors; planning recreational events with other family units
7. Making the most of an indoor playroom or play center.

Each of these headings will be described in some detail.

*Making Routine Activities Fun.* When work is approached in a spirit of fun and cooperation, it loses much of its humdrum quality. Whether the family is engaged in washing dishes, cleaning and opening up a summer camp, painting a house, or any of the many occasional or regular tasks that come up, they may join together in playing lively games (verbal games like Ghost or Geography are most suitable), or singing as they work. In the kitchen there may be a lively rhythm band workout with dishes, pots, and pans as these are washed. Storytelling and guessing or mental games also fit in well while all hands are occupied.

*Developing Common Recreational Interests.* In general this refers to having all members of the family share their hobbies and play interests with each other in an informal, unscheduled way. Several examples of this are mentioned in Chapter 3, and all of the activities mentioned from Chapter 5 on may be carried on jointly by parents and children. Often a father and son will have similar pursuits while mother and daughter develop theirs together. Other interests will appeal to the entire family.

*Regular Family Nights.* Setting aside a regular night or afternoon as often as convenient, is one of the best ways of insuring that parents and

children will get to play with each other. On such a night music may be the
featured activity one week and stunts and dramatic skits the next. One week
it may be games and another week, hobby activity. Often it is fun to use a
tape recorder to record such skits or to prepare "voice-letters" to send to
absent members of the family. Sometimes family nights may be spent
looking at color slides or films of past vacations, or planning future ones in
detail. One approach is to have the first family night of the month Dad's
night, the next Mom's, the next Sis's, etc., with each featured individual
having the right to select his own activity on family night.

One way of drawing the family closer together is to have several family
observances during the year; these may have to do with birthdays, anni-
versaries, important holidays, or events (Jimmy home from camp, etc.).
The family night may be spent in celebrating these highlights of family
living or, in the case of a very special occasion (such as Christmas or an
approaching wedding or graduation), preparing for the event.

Sometimes the family night might be nothing more dramatic than time
spent reading together or to each other or watching favorite television
programs together. The important thing is that each member knows that
*this* night is to be spent with the family and that no other obligations may
interfere.

*Back-yard Fun.* The Eisenbergs suggest many different kinds of activities that may be carried on in the back yard, be it large or small. The
most obvious activities are family picnics and barbecues when the weather
is seasonable. It helps to have a well-equipped area, with such facilities as
an outdoor fireplace or grill (although small portable ones are quite inexpensive). A driveway provides a good spot for game activities; if it is
smooth and large enough, it may be painted with lines for shuffleboard or
deck tennis. Lawn swings, a basketball standard or backboard, a ping-pong
table, horseshoes, croquet, volleyball or badminton nets, jungle gyms, sand-
boxes, and similar kinds of equipment all serve to give the back yard a
rich recreation potential.

In the winter time children may enjoy sledding, ice skating, or skiing
in the back lot if it is spacious enough and has a slope or area that may be
flooded for ice. If not, making a snow man or snow house, cracking the
whip in the snow, building a fort, or playing snow dodge ball are all games
that youngsters enjoy and in which adventurous parents may join them.

Archery is a fine back-yard activity provided that there is a safe back-
stop to prevent stray arrows from winging a sun-bathing neighbor. If there

are enough trees and shrubbery, it may be feasible to have a bird-feeding station and to set up bird houses; watching various families of birds through the spring and summer is a fascinating activity. A good idea is a "Nature Treasure Hunt," in which the family is organized into small teams which must collect various items on a list of objects available in the back yard (such as pine cones, colored stones, ant eggs, flowers, etc.) in a race against each other.

Overnight camping is particularly popular with youngsters, and a pup tent may be pitched in the back yard throughout the summer for this purpose.

Tin cans may be sunk into the lawn to provide a miniature golf course with improvised hazards, traps, and roughs. A regular golf ball, or sometimes a rubber ball or croquet ball, may prove suitable; players may use croquet mallets instead of golf clubs. "Clock Golf," in which twelve stakes are set out like the numbers on a clock, with one "hole" in the center, is another possibility. Indeed there are an infinite number of possibilities for back-yard play.

*Outings and Trips.* Chapter 12 dealt in some detail with forest camping; however, there are many other kinds of trips and excursions that families can go on together, from afternoon outings to journeys taking several weeks. The long hours of travel in autos, busses, or trains may be whiled away by playing mental or guessing games; often these may be tied up to geography to make them more pertinent. The Eisenbergs suggest several automobile games, such as picking a destination and then having a contest spotting license plates of other cars which will get the family to the destination, state by state. Each individual may select a different route and have to spot the license plates of states to get there along the road. This game is best played during the vacation season when there are plenty of cars along the road.

Various other games based on the alphabet or numbers may be played, getting letters or numbers from the license plates of oncoming or passing cars or from roadside signs. These games may pit the front seat against the back seat or those on the right side of the car against those on the left.

Family outings or trips may not all cover a great deal of distance, nor need they always be in the country. The city family will find a wealth of interesting places to go to, such as parks, zoos, and beaches. They may take a trolley or subway trip to the end of the line. They may go to children's theater or concerts and to museums or other exhibitions, such as the

Planetarium. Automobile shows, sports shows, family home shows, and similar expositions are usually fun. The circus and rodeo come to town— and they're a "must" for the family. In large cities there are usually some fascinating foreign sections; the whole family may enjoy visiting Chinatown or having shish-kebab in an Armenian restaurant. Many large factories and industrial plants have guided tours which represent real adventure to youngsters, and in harbor cities it is a delightful (although somewhat smelly) treat to make a predawn visit to the wharves to see the fishing boats coming in or to watch the bustling activity in huge fish markets.

*Special Activities with Family Guests and Friends.* The family, as a unit, may invite and entertain guests from other neighborhoods or cities. All together parents and children may plan the menus and do the cooking or work out plans for entertaining the visitors. Often it is fun to plan joint activities with other families that have children of approximately the same age. Sometimes churches, community clubs, and similar organizations will plan special family parties, with suitable activities for various age levels and, at the end, a big buffet supper and entertainment for all.

*Indoor Play Center.* This room, whether it be in the basement, garage, attic, or elsewhere in the house, should be equipped with a record player, ping-pong table, a sturdy table for crafts, various equipment games, and whatever is necessary to meet the special interests of members of the family. This should be one room in the house that is completely durable and damageproof, if such be possible. Shelves and other storage space should be provided. Ideally it should have a fireplace for sitting around and toasting marshmallows on wintry nights; it would also be convenient to have a small refrigerator or ice-box there, for storing soft drinks or other refreshments. The walls might be covered with travel posters or mounted photographs of family activities. It is also a good idea to keep a family scrapbook here and a guest book, in which those visiting the home may sign their names with some humorous comment on their stay in the house.

## Summary

This chapter outlines the need for parents and children to enjoy play activities together and suggests ways in which families may take stock of their recreational lives. Several emphases for developing family fun are suggested, having to do with the "when," "where," and "how" of jointly shared recreation in and around the home.

# CHAPTER 15

# EVALUATING
# CHILDREN'S PLAY

This book has presented a wide variety of play activities for youngsters, together with guides for their most effective use. From time to time the teacher, recreation leader, or parent who has a real concern about the outcomes of children's play will want to take a good hard look at what is going on—in other words, to evaluate it!

How can he do this?

He might begin by informally observing children at play.

He might attempt to appraise the spirit with which they are participating, their enthusiasm, interest, and absorption.

He might, if the activity involved active sports or games, try to judge the quality of sportsmanship displayed and how rules and group decisions are accepted.

If the activity involved a specific product, as in dramatics or arts and crafts, the adult might judge this tangible evidence of the play experience.

He might consider the apparent relationships existing among the children; are there exclusive cliques and rivalries or does a friendly, democratic, mutual feeling seem to prevail?

He might—and certainly should—talk at length to the children themselves to find out how they feel about the activity.

Beyond all these, it probably would be helpful for him to develop a broad measuring stick against which to measure any play program, whether carried on independently by children or with the assistance of adults.

219

## *Judging the Play Program*

A well-conceived and soundly guided play life for children is likely to include the following attributes:

It will encourage the total growth of the child, including the various aspects that have previously been mentioned, physical, social, emotional, intellectual, and creative. We know today that we cannot consider the child's emotional well-being without taking into account his social experiences. A child who is physically subpar cannot be expected to operate consistently at his intellectual best. These functions and aspects are closely interrelated in play, as in all other phases of life.

Play experiences should be suitably geared to the developmental stages of the child, in that new problems and developmental tasks arise when he is ready to meet them. Children learn best when they are psychologically and physically prepared to solve a particular problem and when the problem is meaningful to them. Generally a developmental task is considered to be one which arises at or about a certain period in the life of the individual, successful achievement of which leads to his happiness and to success with later tasks, while failure leads to unhappiness, disapproval by others, and difficulty with later tasks. In the desirable play program each child is given the chance to tackle the right task at the right time.

Another aspect of sound play activities is that they allow each child a good measure of success. No matter what his skills or talents are, no child should be condemned to continual defeat or frustration. At the same time each youngster should be helped to estimate realistically his own strengths and weaknesses. In time he will learn to accept failure without feeling that he is disgraced or rejected because of it. As a result he should learn to set personal goals that are feasible in terms of his own ability. Many adults function poorly because in childhood they never learned to set their sights at a reasonable level. Either their personal goals (or the goals that were set for them by the pressure of adults or friends) were so high that they could never be met or, lacking confidence, they consistently set their sights too low and never learned how far they could really go. Each child should be encouraged to realize his own potential and to do his best—but should not be allowed to reproach himself for failing to achieve goals that are impossible for him.

In play a child should have the opportunity to take part in many different kinds of activities which will act as challenging and broadening influences in his life. Through dramatic, imaginative play he can envision himself in many lands, settings, centuries, and situations. He can function as farmer, carpenter, athlete, soldier, doctor, artist—all in play. He can take on many group roles, thus enriching his own resources as a person.

There is the question of whether competition or cooperation should be stressed in childhood play, and to what degree. Many adults deliberately tend to stress competitive values and ways of behavior, on the premise that human beings are essentially highly competitive and that their children should learn to battle tooth-and-nail at an early age since they will soon enough be forced to do it in adult life. Bossard comments, "Parents and other adults are prone to encourage child competition . . . and in a form more stark and unrestricted than they employ in their adult relations. Viewed through the eyes of the child, this is a hard world, in which the contestants often are extremely cruel to each other." [63] Who has seen the newsreel of the Little League hurler of eleven or twelve bursting into tears when his final pitch is slammed for a home run that costs his team the league championship? In the soundly conceived recreation program, the goal is to give all children satisfying play experiences. This cannot be done when the sole emphasis is on high-pressure competitive events. The ultimate outcome of happy experiences in childhood play should be to help create stable, secure children who will later be able to operate effectively in all kinds of life situations, whether they are cooperative or competitive.

Play activities should help each child learn to give and take, accept responsibilities, and respect the needs, desires, and opinions of others. He agrees to obey societal restraints and gains the kind of discipline that comes from within because it is recognized as necessary and logical, rather than artificially imposed and enforced. This voluntary, inner discipline is the most effective kind, based as it is on sound understandings between children and adults as to the need for governing behavior.

Most children actually welcome having certain rules and limitations; often what appears to be deliberately destructive behavior is simply an attempt on the part of the child to find out what the real limits are. As evidence of the fact that children usually have high regard for other children who respect rules, surveys of social popularity have shown that one trait of popular youngsters is that they can enter quickly into a group situation and conform to it with an easy, unobtrusive adjustment, obeying the rules that have been set up. On the other hand children who are noisy, boastful, and poorly disciplined usually are among the least popular youngsters in a group.

One of the major values of a good play program is that it endows each child with a sound self-concept in which he has a strong belief in his own worthwhileness, an accurate picture of his own abilities, strengths, and weaknesses, and a solidly based security in his particular sex role.

Usually during the gang age each child finds the greatest security in allying himself with his own sex group and conforming to its code of not associating regularly with members of the opposite sex or respecting their values. Then during the early adolescent years he will go through a stage of peace-making with the opposite sex which develops into the dating period.

If the gang-age segregation of the sexes is too pronounced over too long a time, this may be a difficult transition for children to accomplish. Therefore it is desirable that even during the height of the gang period, when boys and girls may profess undying contempt for each other, there should be some opportunity for them to mingle on a friendly basis. Activities should be chosen that do not emphasize the differences between the sexes (such as body-contact sports), and that do not over-glamorize the idea of romance or dating.

With regard to emotional stability, it has already been pointed out that desirable play practices should give each child a strong feeling of security and acceptance in his group life. Certain projective media may give the child an opportunity to work out his anxieties, antagonisms, conflicts, and tensions.

Implicit in the preceding paragraph is the fact that imagination, fantasy, and make-believe are extremely important aspects of play, particularly for younger children. However, when fantasy begins to become so repeated and systematic that children lose interest in the actual group life around them and weaken the effort and concentration devoted to real play, it is a sign that they are relying on fantasy for satisfaction to an unhealthy degree. Excessive daydreaming may in this way result in marked introversion and separation from the group. To counteract it, socializing forms of play should be stressed and children should be given special help to make sure that their play experiences are as satisfying and rewarding as possible.

It has already been suggested that each child should have the opportunity to develop creative skills, interests, and understandings. This approach emphasizes freeing the child's powers of expression and giving him a creative viewpoint toward all of life's activities and experiences.

When creative activities are carried on in this manner, there is no rigid schedule of materials to be covered or skills to be learned. The awkward, poorly coordinated, bashful, self-conscious, or unexpressive child is helped to enjoy the experience as much as the most highly skilled. At no time is performance or product made a paramount goal, although children are continually helped to develop standards, increase their mastery of the various expressive techniques involved, and move toward self-direction, independent decision-making, and self-appraisal.

A final characteristic of the desirable play program is that it should afford the participants plenty of opportunity for relaxed free play and individual choice of activities. The community center or recreation program that rigidly organizes all activities on a round-the-clock schedule and that has definite expectations about when and how children should take part is not really play-minded.

In a flexible and free program each child may be expected to develop a different cluster of choices and skills and to explore each according to his individual needs and interests. There are no universal expectations; one child may be a good athlete, another an artist, another a mechanic or scientist. In terms of group roles one child may be a fine organizational leader; another, the kind of "idea man" who sparks the group but does not follow through in a practical way. Another may serve as the conscience of the group or as a good, solid follower. There is a place for each kind of child in the play society.

The important need is for an accepting atmosphere to be established in which each child may attain a sufficient degree of success and a confident feeling of acceptance by the group. From this it is hoped that the self-reliant, enthusiastic, adventurous, purposeful, resourceful, and creative child will emerge happier and stronger in every way.

## Summary

This chapter describes several criteria for judging children's play programs. Activities should contribute to the total growth and should be geared to the developmental stages of youngsters. They should provide each child with a variety of experiences and should contribute to his cooperative social behavior and realistic self-concept. Creative experiences and plenty of opportunity for free, relaxed play and individual choice of activities are also important.

# SUGGESTED READINGS

The following books provide helpful background in the broad areas of child development, the role of play, and leadership approaches, as well as in the specific kinds of recreation activities described in this book. Most of the books listed were recently published. A few are older; these may no longer be available from their publishers, but should be obtainable in libraries. The majority of them deal primarily with the six-through-twelve age range. A few which do not, contain some material applicable to children in this range and are therefore listed.

CHILD DEVELOPMENT

Blair, Arthur, and William Burton: *Growth and Development of the Pre-Adolescent,* Appleton-Century-Crofts, Inc., New York, 1951.

Bossard, James: *The Sociology of Child Development,* Harper & Brothers, New York, 1954.

Breckinridge, Marian, and E. Lee Vincent: *Child Development,* W. B. Saunders Company, Philadelphia, 1949.

Gesell, Arnold, and Frances Ilg: *The Child from Five to Ten,* Harper & Brothers, New York, 1946.

Hurlock, Elizabeth B.: *Child Development,* McGraw-Hill Book Company, Inc., New York, 1950.

Millard, Cecil: *Child Growth and Development,* D. C. Heath and Company, Boston, 1951.

Reynolds, Martha May: *Children from Seed to Saplings,* McGraw-Hill Book Company, Inc., New York, 1951.

Strang, Ruth: *An Introduction to Child Study,* The Macmillan Company, New York, 1951.

224

## THE ROLE OF PLAY

Boettiger, Elizabeth: *Children's Play, Indoors and Out,* E. P. Dutton & Co., New York, 1938.

Cunningham, Ruth, and Associates: *Understanding Group Behavior of Boys and Girls,* Bureau of Publications, Teachers College, Columbia University, New York, 1951.

Dulles, Foster Rhea: *America Learns to Play,* New York, Appleton-Century-Crofts, Inc., New York, 1940.

Hutchinson, John: *Principles of Recreation,* The Ronald Press Company, New York, 1949.

Jersild, Arthur, and Ruth Tasch: *Children's Interests and What They Suggest for Education,* Bureau of Publications, Teachers College, Columbia University, New York, 1949.

Lambert, Clara: *Child Care through Play Schools,* Harper & Brothers, New York, 1944.

Mitchell, Elmer, and Bernard Mason: *The Theory of Play,* The Ronald Press Company, New York, 1948.

Nash, J. B.: *Philosophy of Recreation and Leisure,* The C. V. Mosby Company, St. Louis, 1953.


## GROUP LEADERSHIP

Corbin, Dan: *Recreation Leadership,* Prentice-Hall, Inc., Englewood Cliffs, N. J., 1953.

Coyle, Grace: *Group Work with American Youth,* Harper & Brothers, New York, 1948.

Kraus, Richard: *Recreation Leader's Handbook,* McGraw-Hill Book Company, Inc., New York, 1955.

Reiley, Catherine: *Group Fun,* Dodd, Mead & Company, Inc., New York, 1954.

Roberts, D. M.: *Leadership of Teen-Age Groups,* Association Press, New York, 1950.

Slavson, S. R.: *Creative Group Education,* Association Press, New York, 1937.

Vannier, Maryhelen: *Methods and Materials in Recreation Leadership,* W. B. Saunders Company, Philadelphia, 1956.

Stone, Walter, and Charles Stone: *Recreation Leadership,* The William-Frederick Press, New York, 1952.

Wittenberg, Rudolph: *The Art of Group Discipline,* Association Press, New York, 1951.


## GAMES, STUNTS, AND MIXERS

Bauer, Lois, and Barbara Reed: *Dance and Play Activities for the Elementary Grades* (2 vols.), Chartwell House, Inc., New York, 1952.

Borst, Evelyn: *The Book of Games for Boys and Girls,* The Ronald Press Company, New York, 1953.

Depew, Arthur: *The Cokesbury Stunt Book,* Abingdon Press, Nashville, 1953.

Eisenberg, Helen, and Larry Eisenberg: *The Pleasure Chest,* The Parthenon Press, Nashville, 1949.

Frankel, Lillian, and Godfrey Frankel: *101 Best Games for Girls, 101 Best Action Games for Boys,* Sterling Publishing Co., Inc., New York, 1953.

Fraser, Phyllis, and Edith Young: *A Treasury of Games, Quizzes and Puzzles,* Grosset and Dunlap, Inc., New York, 1947.

Geri, Frank: *Illustrated Games and Rhythms for Children,* Prentice-Hall, Inc., Englewood Cliffs, N. J., 1955.

Hindman, Darwin: *Handbook of Active Games,* Prentice-Hall, Inc., Englewood Cliffs, N. J., 1955.

Hunt, Sarah, and Ethel Cain: *Games the World Around,* The Ronald Press Company, New York, 1941.

Mason, Barnard, and Elmer Mitchell: *Social Games for Recreation,* The Ronald Press Company, New York, 1935. (Also published in the Barnes and Noble Everyday Handbook Series as *Party Games for All*).

Mulac, Margaret, and Marian Holmes: *The Party Games Book,* Harper & Company, New York, 1951.

Ripley, G. S.: *The Book of Games,* Association Press, New York, 1952.

FOLK AND SQUARE DANCES, SINGING GAMES, AND PLAY PARTIES

Bauer, Lois, and Barbara Reed: *Dance and Play Activities for the Elementary Grades* (2 vols.), Chartwell House, New York, 1952.

Chase, Richard: *Hullabaloo and Other Singing Folk Dances,* Houghton Mifflin Company, Boston, 1949.

Chicago Park District: *The Square Dance,* Burnham Park, Chicago, 1940.

Duggan, Anne, Jeanette Schlottmann, and Abbie Rutledge: *The Folk Dance Library* (five vols.), The Ronald Press Company, New York, 1948.

Eisenberg, Larry, and Helen Eisenberg: *. . . And Promenade All,* The Methodist Publishing House, Nashville, 1947.

Harris, Jane, Anne Pittman, and Marlys Swenson: *Dance Awhile,* Burgess Publishing Company, Minneapolis, 1950.

Kirkell, Miriam, and Irma Schaffnit: *Partners All—Places All,* E. P. Dutton & Co., Inc., New York, 1949.

Kraus, Richard: *Square Dances of Today,* The Ronald Press Company, New York, 1950.

LaSalle, Dorothy: *Rhythms and Dances for Elementary Schools,* The Ronald Press Company, New York, 1951.

Rohrbough, Lynn: *The Handy Play Party Book* (five kits), Delaware, Ohio, Cooperative Recreation Service, Delaware, Ohio, 1940.

White, Betty: *Betty White's Teen-Age Dance Book,* David McKay Company, Inc., New York, 1952.

## CREATIVE DANCE AND RHYTHMS

Andrews, Gladys: *Creative Rhythmic Movement for Children,* Prentice-Hall, Inc., Englewood Cliffs, N. J.

Cole, Natalie: *The Arts in the Classroom,* The John Day Company, Inc., New York, 1940.

Dixon, C. Madeleine: *The Power of Dance,* The John Day Company, Inc., New York, 1939.

Evans, Ruth, and Emma Battis: *Childhood Rhythms,* Chartwell House, Inc., New York, 1954.

LaSalle, Dorothy: *Rhythms and Dances for Elementary Schools,* The Ronald Press Company, New York, 1951.

Murray, Ruth: *Dance in Elementary Education,* Harper & Brothers, New York, 1953.

Sehon, Elizabeth, and Emma Lou O'Brien: *Rhythms in Elementary Education,* The Ronald Press Company, New York, 1951.

Waterman, Elizabeth: *The Rhythm Book,* The Ronald Press Company, New York, 1936.

## MUSIC

Barton, Fred: *Music as a Hobby,* Harper & Brothers, New York, 1950.

Boni, Margaret: *Fireside Book of Favorite American Songs,* Simon & Schuster, Inc., New York, 1952.

————: *Fireside Book of Folk Songs,* Simon & Schuster, Inc., New York, 1947.

Coleman, Satis: *Creative Music for Children,* G. P. Putnam's Sons, New York, 1931.

Downes, Olin, and Elie Siegmiester: *A Treasury of American Song,* Alfred A. Knopf, Inc., New York, 1943.

Dykema, Peter: *Twice 55 Games with Music,* C. C. Birchard & Co., Boston, 1924.

Flagg, Marion: *Musical Learning, A Guide to Child Growth,* C. C. Birchard & Co., Boston, 1924.

Hood, Marguerite, and E. J. Schulz: *Learning Music through Rhythm,* Ginn & Company, Boston, 1949.

Krevit, William: *Music for Your Child,* Dodd, Mead & Company, New York, 1946.

Landeck, Beatrice: *Children and Music,* William Sloane Associates, New York, 1952.

Leonhard, Charles: *Recreation through Music,* The Ronald Press Company, New York, 1952.

Lomax, John, and Alan Lomax: *Folk Songs: U.S.A.,* Duell, Sloan and Pearce, Inc., New York, 1947.

————: *Our Singing Country,* The Macmillan Company, New York, 1941.

Myers, Louise: *Teaching Children Music in the Elementary School,* Prentice-Hall, Inc., Englewood Cliffs, N. J., 1950.

Rohrbough, Lynn: Various kits, including songs of many nations and holidays, Cooperative Recreation Service, Delaware, Ohio.

Sandburg, Carl: *The American Songbag,* Harcourt, Brace and Company, New York, 1927.

Seeger, Ruth: *American Folk Songs for Children,* Doubleday & Company, Inc., New York, 1948.

———: *Animal Folk Songs for Children,* Doubleday & Company, Inc., New York, 1950.

Sheehy, Emma: *There's Music in Children,* Henry Holt and Company, Inc., New York, 1947.

Zanzig, Augustus: *Singing America,* C. C. Birchard & Co., Boston, 1940.

———: *Community and Assembly Singing,* M. Witmark & Sons, New York, 1933.


DRAMATIC PLAY

Burger, Isabel: *Creative Play Acting,* The Ronald Press Company, New York, 1950.

Davis, Eugene: *Amateur Theatre Handbook,* Greenberg: Publisher, New York, 1945.

Eisenberg, Helen, and Larry Eisenberg: *The Handbook of Skits and Stunts,* Association Press, New York, 1953.

Fisher, Caroline, and Hazel Robertson: *Children and the Theatre,* Stanford University Press, Stanford, Calif., 1950.

Gross, Edwin, and Nathalie Gross: *Teen Theatre, A Guide to Play Production,* Whittlesey House (McGraw-Hill Book Company, Inc.), New York, 1953.

Lease, Ruth, and Geraldine Siks: *Creative Dramatics in Home, School and Community,* Harper & Brothers, New York, 1952.

Mills, Winifred, and Louise Dunn: *Marionettes, Masks and Shadows,* Doubleday & Company, Inc., New York, 1928.

———: *Shadow Plays and How to Produce Them,* Doubleday & Company, Inc., New York, 1938.

Ward, Winifred: *Creative Dramatics,* Appleton-Century-Crofts, Inc., New York, 1930.

———: *Theatre for Children,* The Children's Theatre Press, Anchorage, Kentucky, 1950.

———: *Stories to Dramatize,* The Children's Theatre Press, Anchorage, Kentucky, 1952.


ARTS AND CRAFTS

Arends, Jack: *Your Child Needs Art,* unpublished paper, Advanced School of Education, Teachers College, Columbia University, New York, 1952.

Gaitskell, C. D.: *Arts and Crafts in Our Schools,* Chas. A. Bennett Company, Inc., Peoria, Ill., 1950.

Griswald, Lester: *Handicrafts,* Prentice-Hall, Inc., Englewood Cliffs, N. J., 1952.

Ickis, Marguerite, and Reba Esh: *Book of Arts and Crafts,* Association Press, New York, 1953.

Jaeger, Ellsworth: *Easy Crafts,* The Macmillan Company, New York, 1947.

Perry, Evadna: *Crafts for Fun,* William Morrow & Company, Inc., New York, 1940.

Staples, Frank: *Arts and Crafts for the Recreation Leader,* National Recreation Association, New York, 1943.

Viola, Wilhelm: *Child Art,* Chas. A. Bennett Company, Inc., Peoria, Ill., 1942.

NOTE: For an extensive mimeographed listing of books in such areas as basketry, block printing, furniture making, leathercraft, pottery and ceramics, puppetry, textile printing and tincraft, a fine source is the Pacific Recreation Service, Box 185, San Jose, California. Operated by Betty and Buford Bush, this service supplies not only books, but craft tools and supplies and recreation leadership training, in these areas of play activity.

## CAMPING AND NATURE STUDY

Donaldson, G. W.: *School Camping,* Association Press, New York, 1952.

Gaudette, Marie: *Leader's Nature Guide,* Girl Scouts of the USA, New York, 1942.

Hammett, Catherine, and Virginia Musselman: *The Camp Program Book,* Association Press, New York, 1951.

Life Camps, Inc.: *Extending Education through Camping,* New York, 369 Lexington Ave., 1948.

Manley, Helen, and M. F. Drury: *Education through School Camping,* C. V. Mosby Company, St. Louis, 1952.

Price, Betty: *Adventuring in Nature,* National Recreation Association, New York, 1951.

Vinal, William: *Nature Recreation,* McGraw-Hill Book Company, Inc., New York, 1940.

Webb, Kenneth, and Susan Webb: *Summer Magic,* Association Press, New York, 1953.

NOTE: See also list of Pacific Recreation Service, Box 185, San Jose, California.

## FAMILY FUN

Bley, Edgar: *Have Fun with Your Son,* W. B. Saunders Company, Philadelphia, 1954.

D'Amico, Victor: *Art for the Family,* Museum of Modern Art, New York, 1954.

Eisenberg, Helen, and Larry Eisenberg: *The Family Fun Book,* Association Press, New York, 1953.

Osborne, Ernest: *The Family Scrapbook,* Association Press, New York, 1951.

Shuttleworth, Dorothy: *Exploring Nature with Your Child,* The Greystone Press, New York, 1952.

# FOOTNOTES

1. Ruth Strang, *An Introduction to Child Study,* The Macmillan Company, New York, 1951, p. 495.
2. Arnold Gesell and Frances Ilg, *The Child from Five to Ten,* Harper & Brothers, New York, 1946, p. 360.
3. Hans Kraus and Ruth Hirschland, "Muscular Fitness and Health," *Journal of American Association for Health, Physical Education and Recreation,* December, 1954.
4. James Bossard, *The Sociology of Child Development,* Harper & Brothers, New York, 1954, p. 545.
5. J. B. Nash, *Philosophy of Recreation and Leisure,* The C. V. Mosby Company, St. Louis, 1953.
6. *What We Like to Do,* New York State Education Department Physical Education Standards Project Bulletin 5, Albany, New York, 1954.
7. Arthur Jersild and Ruth Tasch, *Children's Interests and What They Suggest for Education,* Bureau of Publications, Teachers College, Columbia University, New York, 1949.
8. Strang, *op. cit.,* p. 496.
9. Harriet Blackwell, "Every Community Needs a Place to Have Fun," *Parents' Magazine,* February, 1949.
10. Margaret Hickey, "Recreation Center for a California Town," *Ladies' Home Journal,* April, 1955.
11. John Dewey, *Democracy and Education,* The Macmillan Company, New York, 1921, p. 241.
12. Edwin Trethaway, "Don't Just Turn Them Loose," *Journal of the National Education Association,* April, 1954.
13. Zollie Maynard, "Florida's Summer Program, Choice of 125,000 Children," *A.A.H.P.E.R. Journal,* November, 1953.
14. Dorothy Barclay, "Girl Scouts in Search of Leaders," *The New York Times Magazine,* June 5, 1955.

15. James Hymes, Jr., "Why Play Is Important," *Parents' Magazine,* November, 1949.

16. Jeanne Seiber and C. W. McCullough, "What a Hobby Did for Our Son," *Parents' Magazine,* June, 1954.

17. Walker Tompkins, "An Amazing New Hobby: Ham Radio for the Whole Family," *Parents' Magazine,* February, 1955.

18. Caroline Zachry and Margaret Lighty, *Emotion and Conduct in Adolescents,* Appleton-Century-Crofts, Inc., New York, 1940, p. 280.

19. Dorothy Barclay, "The Men in Children's Lives," *The New York Times Magazine,* June 19, 1955.

20. *Ibid.*

21. Fredric Wertham, *Seduction of the Innocent,* Rinehart & Company, Inc., New York, 1954.

22. Dana Harlow, "Camp Kno-Koma," *Recreation Magazine,* April, 1954.

23. "Recreation Center for the Cerebral Palsied," *Recreation Magazine,* April, 1954.

24. James Herdic, Jr., "Swimming for Handicapped Children," *Recreation Magazine,* Feb., 1955.

25. John Herzog, "Boys and Girls Together, Handicapped and Able-Bodied," *Recreation Magazine,* June, 1955.

26. Clark Moustakas, *Children in Play Therapy,* McGraw-Hill Book Company, Inc., New York, 1953.

27. Charles Baker, "Remedial Recreation in a Child Care Institution," *Recreation Magazine,* November, 1954.

28. "Children in Trouble" (A Forum on Juvenile Delinquency), *Ladies' Home Journal,* March, 1955.

29. Sheldon Glueck and Eleanor Glueck, *Delinquents in the Making,* Harper & Brothers, New York, 1952, pp. 206–7.

30. Grace Coyle, *Group Work with American Youth,* Harper & Brothers, New York, 1948, p. 252.

31. Ruth Cunningham and Associates: *Understanding Group Behavior of Boys and Girls,* Bureau of Publications, Teachers College, Columbia University, New York, 1951, pp. 29–30.

32. Cunningham, *op. cit.,* p. 32.

33. Sam Thomas, "Let Lili Dance," unpublished paper, Teachers College, Columbia University, New York, n.d.

34. Virginia Copeland, unpublished brochure on dance classes.

35. Natalie Cole, *The Arts in the Classroom,* The John Day Company, Inc., New York, 1940.

36. Lucy Mitchell, *Here and Now Story Book,* E. P. Dutton & Co., Inc., New York, 1921.

37. Tom Scott, *Sing of America,* Thomas Y. Crowell Company, New York, 1947, p. 26.

38. C. Madeleine Dixon, *The Power of Dance,* The John Day Company, Inc., New York, 1939.

39. Elizabeth Hayes, *Dance Composition and Production*, New York, Ronald Press, 1955, pp. 11–20.

40. Grace Piskula, "Boys Like Modern Dance, Too" (May, 1954) and, Charlotte Irey, "Men in the College Dance Group" (October, 1955), both in *A.A.H.P.E.R. Journal.*

41. Beatrice Landeck, *Children and Music*, William Sloane Associates, New York, 1952.

42. Howard Murphy, "Music in General Education," *Teachers College Record,* April, 1953, pp. 381–382.

43. Sigmund Spaeth, *The Art of Enjoying Music, Whittlesey House* (McGraw-Hill Book Company, Inc.), 1933, p. viii.

44. Lillian Baldwin, *Music for Young Listeners,* Silver Burdett Company, New York, 1951.

45. David Ewen and Nicolas Slonimsky, *Fun with Musical Quizzes and Games,* Prentice-Hall, Inc., Englewood Cliffs, N. J.

46. Landeck, *op. cit.,* p. 16.

47. Ruth Seeger, *American Folk Songs for Children,* Doubleday & Company, Inc., New York, 1948.

48. Augustus Zanzig, *Community and Assembly Singing,* New York, M. Witmark & Sons, New York, 1933.

49. Peter Slade, *Child Drama,* University of London Press, Ltd., London.

50. Caroline Fisher and Hazel Robertson, *Children and the Theatre,* Stanford University Press, Stanford, 1950.

51. Jack Arends, "Your Child Needs Art," unpublished paper, Advanced School of Education, Teachers College, Columbia University, New York, 1952.

52. Arnold Arnold, *How to Play with Your Child,* Ballantine Books, Inc., New York, 1955, pp. 45–48.

53. G. W. Donaldson, *School Camping,* Association Press, New York, 1952.

54. Elmer Mitchell and Bernard Mason, *The Theory of Play,* Ronald Press, New York, 1948, p. 407.

55. Peter Cardozo, *A Wonderful World for Children,* Bantam Books, Inc., New York, 1956.

56. Horace Coon, *Hobbies for Pleasure or Profit,* New American Library of World Literature, Inc., New York, 1955.

57. "Series of Five Articles on Children's Parties," *Life* magazine, February 6, 1956; March 5, 1956; May 7, 1956; June 11, 1956; July 23, 1956.

58. Mary Breen, *The Party Book,* National Recreation Association, and Ronald Press, New York, 1939.

59. *Recreation Program Aids,* National Recreation Association, New York.

60. Ernest Osborne, *The Family Scrapbook,* Association Press, New York, 1951, p. 201.

61. *Ibid.,* p. 281.

62. Larry Eisenberg and Helen Eisenberg, *The Family Fun Book,* Association Press, New York, 1953.

63. James Bossard, *The Sociology of Child Development,* Harper & Brothers, New York, 1954, p. 444.

# INDEX